Love, Happiness

Easy-to-follow guide to enhancing relationships

Mary Jane Kasliner & Shelley Mengo

ISBN 1- 4196 – 0053 -2

Cover & Interior formatting by
Rend Graphics
www.rendgraphics.com

Published by:
BookSurge Publishing, LLC.
5341 Dorchester Road
Suite 16
North Charleston, SC 29418

Visit our website at www.harmoniousliving4u.com

Introduction

Feng Shui is an environmental science that works with the laws of nature, the heavenly bodies of the solar system, and man himself. To say the least, this is a powerful combination based on the wisdom passed down through the ages by Plato, Pythagoras, Einstein, and all of the historical Earth metaphysicians.

These universal laws are described in detail in the I Ching, one of the greatest philosophical books known to man. So what does this all have to do with love and relationships? By first understanding these principles we then can work with enhancing our space and stimulating an area of our life. However, simply placing a vase of red flowers in your romance area or southwest direction will not make you and your partner rich in love. Feng Shui is powerful but without further effort on your part your chances for a loving relationship will not grow. Remember, the laws that govern the applications of Feng Shui are based on heaven, man, and earth.

If our space is imbued with positive imagery, objects we love, and the power of intention, it will support us and speak our inner desires. It is then we begin to realize our true potential in life, with of course the most important aspect being a loving relationship.

It is with great pleasure that we are able to share our first book Love, Happiness And Feng Shui with you. We invite you to take in the energy of the written words and gain a better understanding of the principles behind this ancient Taoist philosophy and apply them to your space to create a harmonious, loving environment for you and your partner.

Chinese Proverb

If there is harmony in the house, there is peace in the nation. If there is order in the nation, there will be peace in the world.

Blessings!

Mary Jane & Shelley

Acknowledgements

We like to think our business partnership is karmic. Meeting over 16 years ago in a dental office both consulting the dentist in different aspects of the practice operation, is where it all began. Yes, believe it or not, we were dental consultants prior to Feng Shui consultants. It was then we were determined to make a difference in other people's lives. It was also when our writing projects took hold of us. The endless hours of research, missing family time, and yes, even a meal or two. A dental practice manual was the result, but who knew it was the beginning of a new path for us both. This new direction led us down the path to Feng Shui, an intriguing yet unfamiliar road. A decision so right that we never looked back and made the dramatic change in our dental consulting business to becoming Feng Shui facilitators and consultants. From that day forward our focus became Feng Shui.

After just a short period of time as practicing consultants, we decided to undertake the awesome goal of creating and opening a Feng Shui school of our own. With worldwide media coverage by the Associated Press, we found ourselves with yet another task; making our school available for those out of our state and country.

So we have come to realize yet another project, this book. Our love and desire to help others achieve harmony and abundance took hold of us, and once again we found ourselves putting in endless hours at the computer and frantically trying to balance family and work. So it is here that we acknowledge and give heart felt gratitude to our husbands, Ron and Peter, who if not for them putting up with our endless hours of making love to the computer and not them, this book would not exist. Christina, my daughter and at times Shelley's too, experienced the hard work and endless hours many times herself being shuffled here and there so the job could be finished.

Here's to our family and friends who have endured our Feng Shui conversations and over exuberance!

We acknowledge each and everyone of our clients who welcomed us into their homes and lives with open arms and entrusted us with their inner hopes and desires of achieving harmony and abundance on every level in their lives. For without them the mutual learning process would not exist.

For our students who work so diligently at learning this sometimes overwhelming discipline, we are truly thankful. Their steadfast commitment to learning this discipline fills us with such joy and honor. For as we teach them they teach us in return.

Finally, we thank our teachers who put in endless hours themselves to see that we understood the principles of Feng Shui and continue to support us when we need them.

Table Of Contents

1
History Of Feng Shui

Translated in the Mandarin Feng Shui means "Wind" and Water." These are two very powerful elements within the environment that sustains life as we know it. Wind translates into the oxygen we breath into our lungs to nourish our cells and carry out intricate processes within the body.

The human body is made up of 70% water and thus relies on the constant replenishment of this element to keep systems functioning smoothly. So as we can see, the translation of "Feng Shui" has an awesome impact on all living things.

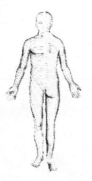

History Of Feng Shui

Where Did It Come From? Feng Shui originated in ancient China thousands of years ago. Men of that time studied the environment, nature, weather patterns and terrain. This is a science known as Geomancy. The earth left behind signs such as wind-worn trees, torpid rivers, meandering streams, jagged rock formations, and rolling hills that were observed to determine the best site location for burial grounds for the wealthy, along with the best site for the emperors palace.

Yin Feng Shui was practiced first, whereby, observing the land topography was essential in choosing the most auspicious site for the ancestral dead. This practice was believed to bless the earthly family members. Yang Feng Shui, widely practiced today, focuses on determining the most auspicious dwelling site for the living.

Later, legend has it, King Hsi witnessed a giant tortoise rising from the Yangtze river inscribed with markings upon its shell. These markings became the interpretation of the Lo Shu or "Magic Square". These markings further developed into the Trigrams of the I Ching, a great philosophical book of changes that describes the workings of the universe. These trigrams are depicted on the Bagua (Bogg-wha) map of life.

When Did Feng Shui Arrive In The United States?

Feng Shui was introduced in the United States during the California Gold Rush of the 1840's. Men came from afar to seek fortunes. Chinese immigrants were part of this mass search for gold and brought their Feng Shui belief system with them. No more than 140 years later, Grand Master Lin Yun put Feng Shui back on the map when he developed a much simpler Western version of Feng Shui that is widely practiced today.

Feng Shui Schools

There are many cultures throughout the world that practice the principles of Feng Shui; however, there are three main schools derived out of the initial art and science.

Form School

This approach examines the land formations and water courses. In ancient Chinese mythology, there are four celestial animals associated with land topography. The ultimate goal was to find a valley-a piece of land protected by these four celestial animal land forms.

1. Green Dragon: This celestial animal is depicted by undulating hills to the eastern side of the dwelling resembling the humps of the dragons back.

2. White Tiger: These hills are lower and stretch out along the western side of the dwelling.

3. Black Tortoise Hills: This is the highest land formation and supports the back of the dwelling to the north.

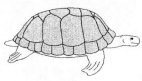

4. Red Phoenix: The Phoenix bird represents a low hill or open space to the south or front of the dwelling.

To top off the site, a meandering river flowing in front of the dwelling cultivates chi and prosperity. Since many of us live in cities, we rarely will have undulating hills surrounding us, but not to fret, a professional Feng Shui practitioner can analyze the buildings and roadways and associate them to the four celestial animals.

Compass School

While the geomancers recorded earth formations, astronomers charted the skies. This information was transcribed onto a special compass known as a Lo Pan. Using the Lo Pan, the Feng Shui master could then harmonize the energy of an individual (astrology) with the energy of their surroundings.

Black Hat Sect

Lo Pan

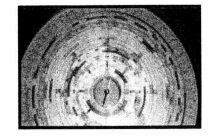

Founded by its spiritual leader, Grand Master Lin Yun, it combines the traditional principles of Feng Shui with spirituality and symbolism. Using the bagua by door entry, this map points out areas of one's life and makes assessments according to the principles of Feng Shui design. This is the most popular method used in the United States, and closely resembles the 12 parted Euro-Bagua system we will undertake in this book.

Chi

Chi is the cosmic breath of life within all of us and everywhere around us. It is what makes the wind blow and the waterways flow. It is believed to permeate all things, and made up of two components, yin and yang. We all possess our own unique form of chi marked by our birth date and time. The essence of Feng Shui is to evaluate how personal chi interacts with environmental chi. If there is stagnation of chi or an overabundance of it, it can be problematic for us. The ultimate goal is to align oneself with auspicious or benevolent chi that will bring about harmony and balance. By doing so, opportunities will open up to us and be easily recognizable where we can use them to our benefit.

5 Elements

The Chinese believe everything is in constant change between the five elements or forces in nature. The five elements are not actually elements but qualities or stages that flux in a continuum or cycle. Wood, Fire, Earth, Metal and Water are the five forces within nature. These forces react to each other in either a productive, weakening, or destructive cycle.

Productive Cycle

The productive or birthing cycle is the most harmonious of the cycles by feeding one element into another. **Water** nourishes the wood or plant, **Wood** feeds the fire, **Fire** burns to create ash or earth, **Earth** contains ore or metal, **Metal** liquefies and flows like water.

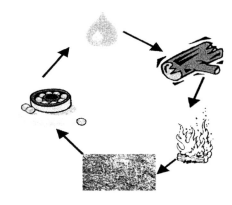

Destructive Cycle

In this phase the elements are not working together. It is a chaotic cycle and can feel like Murphy's Law. **Water** dowses the fire. **Fire** melts the metal, **Metal** (axe) cuts the wood, **Wood** uproots the earth, **Earth** dams the water.

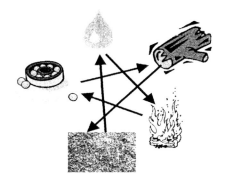

Weakening Cycle

This cycle is very effective in restoring balance back to the birthing cycle. The elements interact by exhausting the element that precedes it. **Water** weakens the metal, **Metal** moves the earth, **Earth** exhausts the fire, **Fire** burns the wood pile, and **Wood** absorbs the water.

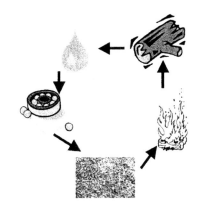

The Elements: Color, Shape And Compass Direction

*E*ach element corresponds to a color, shape and compass direction. This becomes very useful when using Feng Shui design to balance a room.

Wood
The Wood energy is upward and columnar in shape. The color representation is green and the directions are east and southeast.

Earth
Earth energy spins and stabilizes. The shape is square and the color is yellow. The southwest and northeast are the two directions for this element.

Metal
Metal contracts and is circular or oval in shape. The colors are grey, white or gold and the directions are west and northwest.

Fire
Fire energy ascends to the heavens and is triangular in shape. The color is red and the compass direction is south.

Water
Water energy flows downward and is irregular in shape. The colors are black or blue and the direction is north.

Yin And Yang

The Tai Chi symbol represents the concept of yin and yang. They are interdependent forces that drive the world. Yin energy is responsive (female like) and yang energy is dynamic (male like). These forces are in constant motion, whereby, one force tries to dominate the other. The key in Feng Shui is to maintain a balance between these forces so harmony ensues.

Yin	Yang
Dark	Light
Cold	Hot
Soft	Hard
Night	Day
Quiet	Loud
Winter	Summer
Moon	Sun
Downward	Upward

Yin

Yang

The Bagua And Magic Square

The Eastern Bagua is based on the Magic Square. It is given the term "Magic" as every line adds up to the number fifteen. This square exists in many cultures throughout the world, and represents astronomical and geomantic (land form) calculations that are plotted on an intricate Chinese compass, known as a Lo Pan.

The energy always moves in a fixed pattern indicated by the arrows above. These patterns repeat themselves over a period of time (20 year cycles) known as flying star Feng Shui, and can determine prosperity for a person or dwelling in a certain year.

The Magic Square number set was adapted into the 9 palaces and the bagua was derived from these nine palaces.

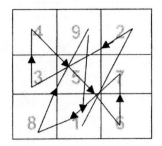

Magic Square

Wood	Fire	Earth
4	9	2
Southeast	South	Southwest
Wood	Earth	Metal
3	5	7
East		West
Earth	Water	Metal
8	1	6
Northeast	North	Northwest

Nine Palaces

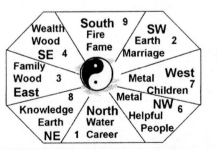

Bagua

The Bagua

The bagua literally means eight parts and represents the human journey through life. Each section represents a compass directional energy associated with the five elements and their colors. This tool has many components to it and we can use it to create a harmonious environment to live and work in.

By taking the bagua and superimposing it over a building, room, or even a desktop, we can map out the areas in our life and how they fall within the building or a room. Following the Black Hat Sect approach, we can overlay the bagua by aligning to the door entry.

Three Gate Entry

By using the three gate entry, we may superimpose the map only through the Career (center), Helpful People (bottom right), or Knowledge (bottom left).

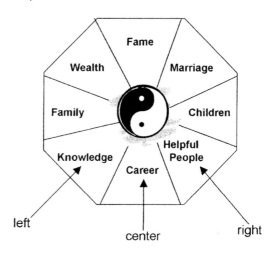

Superimpose Bagua over a building, home or room

12-Parted Euro-Bagua

So how do we arrive at the 12 parted Euro-Bagua? By taking the traditional 8 parted bagua system and applying Western concepts and traditions to it, we establish an intricate road map depicting the life cycle of mankind. Essentially the corners are divided, thereby expanding the 8 parts to 12 parts. Instead of a room or building being divided into 8 parts, we will divide the room or building into 12 parts providing us with more detail in the different aspects of our lives. Each gua or life aspect is based on the 12 astrological zodiac signs, symbols that are quite familiar to those born and raised here in America.

Why 12 Parts?

Without getting into a very detailed dissertation as to why the East and West differ, the basis of Western antiquity is tied very closely to astrology or the 12 zodiac signs. Furthermore, the West bases much of its distinction on the number 12 as reflected in our measurement of time, the calendar and compass direction.

Since imagery and symbolism is so much a part of Feng Shui, if we do not understand the symbols because of cultural differences, then the impact will not be as profound, and as a result the ultimate success we reap in the way of cures and remedies will be minimal. Confining ourselves to one approach in practicing this art and science is somewhat rigid in thinking.

The Euro-Bagua

The Euro-Bagua divides a wall into three sections; therefore, four walls multiplied by three sections gives us 12 parts. The front aspect (8-12), represents the social aspect of our lives, whereas the back sections (2-6), represent the more personal side of our lives. The Euro-Bagua can be superimposed over a building or room by using door entry or aligning it with compass direction as noted on the inner sections.

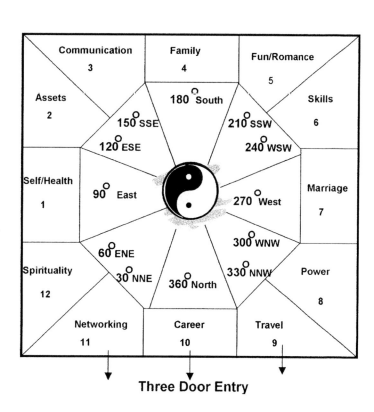

Three Door Entry

The Guas

*A*s you may have noticed, the Euro-Bagua has life stations or guas in slightly different positions from the classical 8 parted system. Once again, this is a cultural distinction. We find using the Euro-Bagua for our clients brings about tremendous changes and believe it is primarily due to the Western culture for which we are applying these principles to. So, now that we have this tool to work with, let's give you some ideas on how to address these sections within your space.

Section 1: *T*his area is the middle third of the far left wall when you enter a room. Since this area represents the east direction it spews vitality and new beginnings. It represents our health on a genetic level and our self image. Therefore, if we are addressing it for health reasons, place an image that spews vitality like a field of sunflowers or a well rooted plant. If you are choosing to portray your ultimate self-

image, then perhaps a sculpture of a Goddess or someone you aspire to be is the symbol of choice. It also represents the astrological sign of Aries, so head images work really well along with any of the fire colors, but red is the best color representation here as it pulls from the red energy of Mars planetary rulership.

Section 2: Located at the far third of the left wall, this section represents the true assets of our wealth. We're talking about your stock portfolio, funds and real estate. Taurus is the zodiac sign with Venus rulership representing stability and beauty of the land. Therefore landscapes, ivy, spider, or money plants work well. Green is the color to strive for here, and when it comes to the artwork, try to keep it original and avoid abstracts as we want our resources to be based on reality.

Section 3: This area is located at the left third of the back wall. It also represents a portion of our wealth and resources. It is the money in our pocket we spend on daily living and hopefully a little extra to invest on some great real estate transaction. Gemini is the zodiac sign which is quite playful and rather energetic. It is an area about communication based on the ruling planet of Mercury, so we like objects with reflectivity and or movement to them. What does this mean? Mirrors, metal chimes, a silver platter propped on an easel or anything that represents communication. Metallic colors such as silver or gold resonate very comfortably in this section as well.

Section 4: *T*his area is located in the middle third of the back wall. It represents our family roots and heritage. It is a very nurturing section as Cancer is the zodiac sign and is ruled by the Moon. This is where you hang the family photos, place the family heirlooms and of course a lovely water fountain, since cancer is a water sign. The creamy whites and pastels are the color choices when working with this sector of the bagua.

Section 5: *T*he right third of the back wall is where you will find this fun section. It is the time of summer where the romance begins and whirlwind affairs take place. We suggest placing pairs of objects and romantic images here to attract that special someone. The pinks, reds, greens, and mauves are all colors of love and therefore work well here. It is the ultimate yang as the Sun rules the astrological sign of Leo, so dynamic is a key ingredient when placing imagery here.

Section 6: *T*he far third of the right wall represents our daily working skills and developed talents. Here is where the attention to detail shines with Virgo as the zodiac sign with Mercury rulership. Herbs, tools, musical instruments, pastel greens or miniature collections all work well in addressing this gua. It also can house pairs of objects as it is an area related to the engagement period of courting. So go ahead and continue with romantic objects to lure that special someone to the alter in the next section!

Section 7: *M*iddle third of the right wall is where you find the section for partnership and marriage. Now it's time to put the contractual agreement together and place the official seal on it. Think pairs and romance here. This is where the wedding portrait is hung and the photo album is stored. Libra is the zodiac sign ruled by Venus. That's right, fairness and love are two essential ingredients when it comes to a lifetime partnership in marriage.

Section 8: *N*ear third of the right wall in a room is where you will find this secretive yet seductive section. Scorpio is the astrological sign ruled by Mars and Pluto. This area is all about power and cooperative ventures. It is also isolating in its position in relation to the rest of the room, and of course with a little help from Pluto kicks it up a notch. The fun thing about this gua is you have many choices when addressing it. A seductive image, garnet colors or desolate piece of artwork like Ansel Adam's winter scenes, or Georgia O'Keefe's desert scenes or sensual flowers all work well. But don't stop there! You can also place any image that represents a cooperative venture such as mountain climbers assisting one another or you can place a water image or fountain here as Scorpio is the second water sign on the Euro-bagua. If you're totally undecided you do not have to address it at all. That's the beauty of the planet Pluto, desolate!

Section 9: *T*his section is located at the right third of the front wall. We are now exposing ourselves to the outer world with a possible door entrance here. This is an area of travel and higher education. Sounds like a dose of optimism is in order here and who better to show it than Sagittarius with Jupiter rulership. Any educational books or objects from other cultures is the ticket to addressing this section. A splash of orange, yellow, or red will do just fine here. If your interest lies in traveling and you have the room, be sure to store your suitcases here.

Section10: *S*mack in the middle of the front wall is where you will find many grand door entrances. This is the section of Capricorn and Saturn. It is our career, our face to the world and image of our father. Place grand images of power and strength here such as bridges, mountains or a grandfather clock. Think the color of wood from your light woods of yellow to dark shades of brown to enhance this section.

Section 11: The left third of the front wall houses the most unusual energy of the entire Euro-Bagua. This is the eccentricity of Uranus that rules the sign of Aquarius. It represents the daily cash that hopefully is pouring into your home or business. Liven this area up with abstract art; the stranger the better. Images of people gathered together and socializing also works well here as it is the area of networking in the community. If your stuck on choosing a color for this area, not to worry as any color will do.

Section 12: Near third of the left wall is the final gua of the 12 parted system. It represents our wisdom, spirit, goals and dreams. It is Pisces ruled by Neptune and Jupiter. This is the third and final water sign on the Euro-Bagua and thus can house a water element. The color purple aligns with spirituality and meditation. Your religious icons, books, and other images of deep meaning fit comfortable into this section.

So here we have a brief analysis of the 12 parted Euro-Bagua map of life. From here on in we will be referring to this system for making our adjustments and cures. The premise of this book is to focus on love and romance, thus these guas will be closely scrutinized to attract that special someone into your life.

2
Sleep Deprivation

Sleep Deprivation

Sleep deprivation has become a big problem with personal and social relationships. Sleep is as important to the human body as food and water, but most of us don't get enough sleep. Our technology and fast pace society has caused much of this problem. Everyone needs at least 6-8 hours of sleep each day to revive brain cells and other body systems so they function effectively.

We have an internal body clock called a circadian clock that controls our natural sleeping pattern. It regulates body hormone levels, heart rate and other vital body functions. When someone suffers from sleep deprivation these important functions become impaired, overall health is affected, not to mention making us moody and forgetful.

We lose sight of this and end up making our bedroom an exercise room, an office, a TV room, and even a room designed for one. To implement Feng Shui recommendations in the bedroom and create a healthy environment is to make us look and feel better which is a plus for good romantic and sensual activities.

We selected some case scenarios depicted in the sleepless bedroom slide that most of us can relate to.   If at least one of these pictures look familiar to you and you are having a problem sleeping, or just wish to have a healthier bedroom, here are some ideas to remedy these Feng Shui faux pas.

Sleepless Bedroom

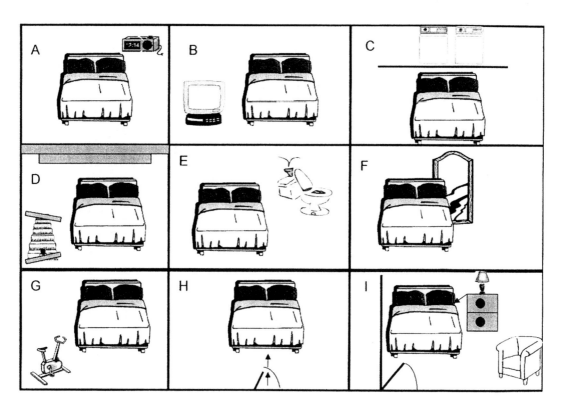

23

Clock Radio (EMF'S)

A

*T*wo reasons why clock radios are problematic; One is the artificial illuminating light source that shines from the face at night, and secondly it runs on an alternating current or an AC electromagnetic field. All electronic devices emit electromagnetic fields that can harm your health.

*A*t night when we are sleeping our body is more sensitive to light and electromagnetic fields than when we are awake and active during the day. Because of this, any EMF source around our body has potential harmful effects and can cause interrupted sleep patterns. Our bodies are designed with a DC current (direct current), smooth movement in one direction that mimics the earth. An AC current alternates direction 60 times per second. The only thing that has an AC current in nature is lightning. I don't know about you but we prefer to be far away when lighting strikes. On the following pages we will delve deeper into the mechanics of electromagnetic frequencies, but for now suffice it to say that it is not something we want in the bedroom!

*D*uring our consultations when we enter bedrooms and see that alarm clock radio by the bedside we cringe. We prefer you toss it out the window but we understand that it will take some time adjusting to the empty spot on your night stand. If you must keep the clock radio in the bedroom, be sure it is at least six feet away from your body. After all, the idea is to get up when the alarm goes off. Using a battery operated alarm clock works in the same fashion but is healthier for a good night sleep.

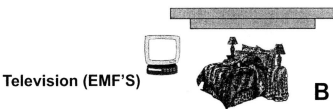

Television (EMF'S)

B

*S*leep is vital to your health and it determines how well you function in your day. When you are ready to retire to the bedroom for the evening, you should never have anything in there to disrupt your sleep except for your partner. Once you place your Feng Shui remedies in this room your disruption by your partner should be a welcoming one.

*T*V's or other electronic items are not good to keep in your bedroom. They will give you sleepless nights because of their harmful exposure, not to mention keeping you from having quality time with your significant other. Remember, magnetic fields are created where electric current is flowing. Unfortunately, the TV is something that many people insist on having there. What you need to realize is that it produces too much energy which disturbs sleep patterns. Not only because of the electromagnetics emanating smog radiation, but when you turn off your TV set at night the glass becomes reflective like a mirror.

*O*ur first recommendation is to take the television out of the room and put it in the guest room along with that exercise equipment. If you are not ready for that change, then enclose it in an entertainment center or cover the screen with a blanket at night. We also strongly suggest placing a smog buster tab on top of the TV. These products remove environmental stress to allow the body to resume to normal functions.

*H*ere's a helpful piece of information; if you do something for 21 days it becomes habit. So, if you no longer view the TV from the bedroom, after 3 weeks it will be like you never had it there.

Beams **B**

*C*hi needs to meander and flow around things that are round or curved. Chi can not flow over right angles or straight objects. Structures such as beams are oppressive and disrupt the natural flow of chi creating a rain effect when it tries to travel. Picture rain pouring down with great force. Now replace the rain with the pressure of chi traveling forcefully downward hitting anyone that lies in its path. Beams emit a suppressive, negative sha energy creating stress and therefore are considered bad for health. They also affect the progress of people who spend a lot of time sleeping or working beneath them. Beams in a bedroom contribute to stress and tension which leads to health issues and relationship problems. The bedroom focus is health and romance, two very important issues we want to improve upon in this particular space.

*T*he obvious solution in this scenario is to remove the beams, and that may mean calling in a contractor. We don't like to advise people to reconstruct their house if they don't have any previous plans on doing so. Luckily for Feng Shui there are inexpensive solutions that we can recommend to abate this problem. If you can't remove them, then paint them the same color as the ceiling so they blend in. Secondly, hang a crystal so the light can generate and activate positive chi energy, taking the stress away from the person underneath them.

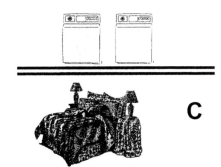

C

Appliances

There are many reports that suggest electromagnetic fields (EMFs) have a negative effect on our immune system. These studies indicate a direct correlation between headaches, cancers, blood disorders and a host of autoimmune diseases when exposed repeatedly to these frequencies.

Appliances below us and above us have an effect on our health. Be especially aware of what is going on opposite the wall your head is positioned when you are asleep. Washers, dryers, refrigerators or any other appliances emit emf's and transmit through the walls. It is during sleep that you are most vulnerable to energy imbalances. That means your bedroom will have the greatest impact on your health. The back of the appliance is the strongest because it is where the motor is built in. You are affected in direct proportion to their strength, proximity, and the length of time you are exposed to these fields. The affect is not instant, it is cumulative. You may notice, if you are in this situation, that you have been experiencing insomnia or anxiety and trying to find a reason why.

Our recommendation is to place a resonator on the appliance and then move the bed to another wall if at all possible. Remember what we told you about direction. Look for the north wall first or other directions other than a south one. If you can, try unplugging the appliance when you're sleeping. If it isn't running it no longer emits EMF's.

Electromagnetic Fields

Electromagnetic fields (EMF's) are present everywhere in our environment but are invisible to the human eye. We are consistently being bombarded by them. There is an electrical field that is present and a magnetic field sometimes present. As consultants, we test the fields and determine how far they go out. We use a tool called a milligauss meter. The meter combines magnetic, electric and radio/microwave detectors, has an easy-to-read needle, and operates on a 9 volt battery. **Electrical fields** are created by differences in voltage: Wires are shielded so the current becomes diminished.

Magnetic fields are created when a device is turned on and the electric current flows: the greater the current, the stronger the magnetic field. This field will penetrate walls, floors or any other common structures. Our nervous system is made up of tiny electrical pulses. The human body is about 70% water and contains salt. This makes us very conductive. Coming in contact with manmade frequencies **(AC current)** over a period of time from things such as power lines, X-rays machines, household appliances, cell phones, clock radios, TVs, fluorescent lighting, computers, and the list goes on, our bodies become disrupted causing symptoms such as fatigue, migraine headaches, stress, sleep disorders, infertility, and chronic disease.

Unfortunately we don't have control of the outside environment, but we do have control of our inside environment, and that means our homes and place of business. You can use your environment as a tool for manifesting what you want; one of them being a healthy space . We want to introduce to you some wonderful products that can do just that. They are special tabs that are made up of cobalt and other space aged materials that absorb and rebroadcast the electric and or magnetic energies in a beneficial form that our bodies can tolerate.

Feng Shui is an environmental science that teaches us how to protect ourselves and improve our health so we can function like our bodies are meant to function. If we feel good we will do everything better, and that brings us back to the premise of this book; feeling energetic to incorporate romance back in your lifestyle.

Products for EMF'S

The products we use and sell from Biomagnetic Research Inc. are truly amazing. This company is the developer of advanced ceramics for electronic pollution clearing. Each product has its specific uses and they all perform amazingly well in removing harmful aspects of electrical as well as magnetic and geopathic energies.

Lets talk a little about these must have products. You may wonder where you should use them. Most homes and businesses have electrical service boxes with circuit breakers and hot water heaters that are generally in the basement or beneath work areas. Spiral energies are emitted affecting the well-being of anyone working or sleeping both near them and above them. These two items are the most important to neutralize. In some cases where people are extremely sensitive, this magnetic energy can be felt on the second floor of a home.

Other items that require these ceramic tabs are: wired appliances, telephones, computers, fluorescent lighting, refrigerators, wireless and microwave devices such as the ever so popular cell phones, microwaves, in house mini-dish entertainment box, wireless home security units, and wireless electronic routers. In addition, any of your battery powered devices such as the engine from automobiles, trains and commercial aircrafts, should have a tab when you are exposed to them frequently or for long periods of time. I am a very energetic person but when I am riding in a car within 15 minutes or so I begin to feel very drained and want to fall asleep. I place the tri-pak in the glove compartment pointed at the engine and have found driving in the car long distances bearable. Whether your traveling for business or for pleasure, and your travel requires the airplane, try packing one in your carryon or placing it under the seat in front of you since most of the wiring of the aircraft runs under the floor beneath you. You'll find this protects you from jet lag.

To learn more about what products are available and the benefits each one has on our health, please visit our website at www.harmoniousliving4u.com.

D

Staircases

*S*taircases are designed for people to go up and down and because of this, the chi or energy is constantly moving. When a staircase is aligned with a bedroom door, that chi or energy becomes negative chi or sha chi, not to mention the strength it takes on. Chi likes to flow around round corners and curves, not straight lines. Straight lines will cause the chi to travel quickly and forcefully instead of meandering the way it should.

*T*he effect on the person sleeping in this room causes negative energy. Depending on where the person is being hit by the sha chi will determine some of the symptoms that will occur. You may find yourself arguing, having neck pain, back tension, foot problems, low energy, dizziness, sinus allergies or other sleeping disorders. Our suggestion for this scenario is to move the bed and command the door. If you move the bed and can not command the door, then position a mirror so you will be in command. The idea is not to feel vulnerable. As long as your body subconsciously knows at a glance it can see the door, you will rest more comfortably. It is important to place the head of the bed on the north wall simply because of the electromagnetic flow of the earth energies from the north pole. If the north wall is not convenient, then place the bed on any of the other compass directions, but never on a south, southeast or southwest wall. These directions are opposite of the magnetic flow of the north pole and will eventually flip your fields making you very tired, causing symptoms like stomach problems and nervous disorders.
One more healthy suggestion, try to keep the head of the bed on a solid wall. Positioning the bed cattycorner allows for chi to swirl around behind you and upset your sleep.

Bathroom Energy

  E

Ancient Chinese homes didn't have bathrooms and toilets to worry about. In Feng Shui there really isn't a good place for a bathroom in a house but we can't get rid of them. Here in the West this is not the case nor is it very practical. I don't think any of us want to go outside to do our business. Most architects like to add an attached bathroom to the master bedroom. We love convenience but don't think about problems that we can have when adding those conveniences.

Bathrooms are very yin and the plumbing has a draining affect on our energy. Energy is important in a bedroom because it encourages relaxation. If you happen to have a bathroom in your bedroom then you need to keep the toilet cover and seat down as well as the drains and doors closed. If you ignore these suggestions you may find yourself waking up several times over the course of the night to use the facility. You may also think about hanging a mirror on the door facing outwards to bring in the view from opposite the bathroom. Do not do this if the bathroom is directly across from you because the mirror will be too energetic with chi that will disturb your sleep, not to mention you will see your reflection in the glass.

Our recommendations are to keep your bathrooms very clean and tidy. Bathrooms do fall in one of your life stations on the bagua, so address them accordingly. Decorate to make them look very luxurious by using gold or brass fixtures. You want your guest to be so comfortable that they don't want to leave the bathroom. Doors always need to be kept closed, because after all, who wants to see a toilet; not too appealing.

We also suggest taping your pipes with red electrical tape three times around. Be sure you are taping under the sink where the pipe meets the bottom of the basin. The other pipes in the bathroom where the toilet is should also be taped. Be sure you tape as close to the pipe where the water comes in from the wall. Red holds positive energy to itself, so symbolically the water will be retained and your wealth will not be flushed away.

F

Mirrors

Mirrors have many uses in Feng Shui. They bring pleasant views into a room, give the illusion of larger space, create missing corners or quas, activate stagnant energy in dark corners and hallways, and deflect negative energy.

Mirrors should be properly used in your space. If they are going to reflect your image they should be in one piece and hung high enough so as not to cut off the head of the tallest person in the household. Sectional mirrors give the illusion of the body being cut into pieces and can have a negative effect on the body parts being cut. However, if you are using them for the sole purpose to reflect light, then the sectional mirror is fine. In terms of shape, round mirrors are recommended because they are auspicious whereas octagonal mirrors are exceptionally powerful.

In the scenario depicted above, your sleep may be disturbed as mirrors move the energy in a room around. In addition, it is believed that the soul does astral traveling while you're sleeping and for it to see its image in a mirror may startle it. Finally, if the view that is reflected in the mirror is less than pleasant, you will be introducing negative energy into your bedroom.

Having mirrors in the bedroom is not advisable since they are too energetic. We know as part of the bedroom furniture our bureaus have mirrors attached to them, but they should never be directly in front of the bed, especially if they will reflect any part of your body while you're in bed.

Gym Equipment

Exercise Equipment – *M*any people use their bedrooms as an exercise room. When your looking at your bike what does it make you think of? Relaxation or activities? When you store workout equipment in your bedroom you bring in the energy of hard work and exertion to your romance. We don't want to constantly feel we are working at having a good relationship.

*I*f you have fold up equipment don't be tempted to slide it under your bed. Not only are you blocking the chi from flowing and supporting your room, your subconscious mind will be thinking of your exercise routine and never allow the body to fully relax and sleep.

*O*ur suggestion for this scenario is to move that equipment in any extra room including your guest room. Don't worry about disturbing your guest and their restful sleep. In Feng Shui, if you make your guests too comfortable they may become your roommates.

*I*n the case of dwellings lacking space, place a screen or a cover over the equipment to keep it from your vision at night. Think romance only and decorate in yin colors, romantic images, dim lighting and room for two.

H

Bed/Door Alignment

*T*he commanding position doesn't mean that the bed should sit in the direct line of the path of the doorway. If your bed does sit in the direct line of the door, the chi entering runs directly and too powerfully up the middle of the bed. This factor can create foot problems to include surgery and possible diseases along the midline of the body for whoever is sleeping here. The feet facing the doorway entrance is also considered the "coffin position" in Feng Shui because this is how the dead were carried out; feet first. Think of how we carry out the coffin in funeral homes. Same way, feet first.

*T*he solution is to move the bed and still try to command the door. If you can not move the bed for any reason, then it is recommended to have a bed with a foot board and also to place a solid object such as a chest in front of the bed to slow down the chi and divert it away from the feet. Crystals are very powerful and the calming stone we suggest is the rose quartz. Place this stone under the mattress at the foot of the bed to soften the flow of chi. Of course another solution is to close the bedroom door. This also serves as a safety procedure in case of fire during the night.

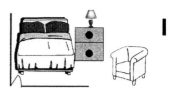

Room for One

If It seems you're forever single or having a problem attracting the right partner, you might consider rearranging this bedroom by allowing room for two. This scenario depicts a bedroom set up for a single person. Looking in this room we see one night-stand, one lamp, a single chair in the partnership section and one way to get into the bed. This bedroom isn't too open to incorporating another person in their lives. Bedrooms project a person's intention around a relationship, so we need to Feng Shui them to allow our prospective partner or our significant other to feel welcome.

*T*his would also hold true if you were married. The person who is sleeping up against the wall will most likely have the least to say in the relationship. The person with most of the space becomes the dominating partner.

*W*e always want to see equality in a bedroom. Our recommendation is a queen size bed positioned in the center of a wall, preferably north direction, allowing for equal distance on either side of the bed. We also like to see two of the same nightstands and lamps if you choose to have them in your decor.

*T*he reason why we mention a queen size bed over a king is that a king has two box springs to be used side by side. This generates a split in the relationship and alters the possibility of the people who sleep in this bed to be together. Don't worry, if you choose not to replace your king size bed our Feng Shui recommendation is to use red silk or satin material beneath the center of the mattress to symbolically bring the chi together preventing separation between the couple.

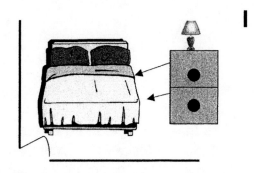

Room For One

One other important factor to recognize in this picture is the positioning of the night stand. We need to be careful when arranging furniture by looking with a critical eye and noticing what may be disturbing to our sleep. The right angles on this piece of furniture is sending negative sha chi to the body. Lay on your bed and see if you are in direct alignment with a "poison arrow", which is any sharp corner that is aimed toward your head, shoulder, knee or any other part of the body.

All this negative energy will disturb your rest and cause health issues, not to mention aches and pains. Generally, one of our suggestions would be to drape a plant to soften this negative chi from the right angle. Since the sha chi is coming off the night stand a plant would not be advisable because it is too close to the bed.

We love plants as Feng Shui remedies but need to be careful when placing them in the bedroom. Two things to keep in mind, plants purify the air but they also need and use up oxygen. Limit one plant that is no more than 3 to 4 feet in height and six feet away from the bed. So our recommendation in this case would be to place a red dot under each of the corners of this night stand. Red draws positive yang energy towards itself therefore neutralizing or deactivating the problematic area.

Purpose of the Bedroom

We spend at least one-third of our lives in the bedroom. This makes it one of the most important rooms of the home. Your bedroom is a place of rest, privacy, intimacy and refuge. If this room is not a place of harmony, the negative energy will harm your marriage, your home life and your physical well-being. Therefore, the effective implementation of Feng Shui in bedrooms is vital to improve the quality of our lives. This room should feel safe, serene and secure because it is here where we rest from the labors of the day, and to allow the body to prepare for the following day. Therefore, a good night's sleep is imperative.

As Feng Shui practitioners, the first thing we take notice of is the health section on the bagua for this room. From the door entrance it's the middle third of the left wall. If you use a compass for the direction then it is 90 degrees east. We need to ask ourselves, does it resonate with healthy, vital images? If your health section is a window, what is outside that window? Is the view healthy plants? Are they evergreens that stay green and healthy all year round or are they prickly rose bushes or holly trees? In Feng Shui everything is literal. So keep pointed sharp plants away from your health area unless you want to be stabbed. We should never compromise our health so never allow foliage to die off. Green, soft, healthy all year round is the Feng Shui remedy. Affirmations are a great tool and are recommended to bring about change in ones life. Write about how you see your health and the health of your partner. You can tuck it away in a draw or behind a picture. Even though it is not viewed, you and the universe both know it is there.

We don't stop there when it comes to our health, we take a look at other interferences that disturb our sleeping pattern. Electromagnetics, gym equipment, reflective items such as too many mirrors are all detrimental to our health.

We also Feng Shui the bedroom for love & romance. This room is to strengthen the relationship between partners or to be addressed to allow a relationship in.

*P*eople who are mentally and physically fit are more likely to have good sex lives. Keeping a fit mind and body can increase your enjoyment of bedroom antics. If you feel good about yourself, you are in a better position to feel good about relationships. When one is not feeling well, and is exhausted, it can certainly have a negative impact on the quality of one's sex life.

*T*he areas we address are the right side of the room. This is about romance, having fun, partnership, sharing and commitment. If you're married then your wedding album would like to cuddle here. To enhance your relationship, a photo of the two of you at heart level with an affirmation on how you see your relationship blossoming is recommended.

*A*ffirmations are very powerful tools for transformation and self-empowerment. By the use of affirmations we can achieve positive relationships and improve our health. If the affirmations are only done half-heartedly, those are the results that will be received. But if a person believes completely in achieving the goal stated in the affirmation, then the situation is almost sure to be achieved.

*W*e are very firm believers that if you ask something of the universe your words will be heard and you will receive. We also believe you must be specific but practical. A typical human trait is to promise ourselves that we will do things to improve our life but almost never carry it out. A large part is because we don't write our goals down. If we write down what we want from our partner, or what we want to see in a relationship, or how we see our health, then it will come to fruition. The power of affirmations is only limited by the person's personal conviction and belief that the affirmations are working.

*S*ample affirmations have been included in the next chapter for you to read and use if you like. Human energy is the most powerful energy of all, so we suggest you try writing affirmations on your own. Place your affirmation about romance in the southwest direction of your bedroom and in the middle third of your right wall preferable at heart level. The southwest being the romance direction and the middle third right wall being the partnership or marriage section of the bagua. Remember, when we direct you to these quas it is always from the door entry of any room. When we mention direction that's when you will use your compass. Don't limit yourself to the romance areas when it comes to affirmations. Place them in any life station to enhance or improve your life.

3
The Power Of Affirmations

The Power Of Affirmations

Affirmations are positive statements of what you want, not what you don't want in your life. Think carefully of the words you chose and write it in the present tense. Remember, an affirmation isn't what your life is about now, it's about how you want your life to be.

Some people have difficulty writing affirmations simply because they may believe they are not worthy of having positive things in their life. Many times we are told that we must struggle to get the finer things in life. It is especially difficult to break this belief system as many times it is drilled into our psyche from an early age. Since thoughts influence our responses to life and our relationships, it behooves us to think positively. We always tell our clients to think about what they want to improve in their life and write an affirmation to support the Feng Shui cure or remedy. Words are very powerful and once you put them down on paper you take them out of the thought process world and put them into reality.

Take the time to read through the many affirmations we included in this chapter. You can use the ones we provided or make up your own. Be creative and enjoy the process, as the power of intention is part of the Feng Shui application.

"He who has conquered doubt and fear has conquered failure. His every thought is allied with power and all difficulties are bravely met and wisely overcome. Thought allied fearlessly to purpose becomes creative force."

**James Allen -
from "As A Man Thinketh"**

Affirmations For Relationships

*B*elow is a list of positive affirmations that you can place in the southwest direction or far right corner of your bedroom via door entry along with the appropriate symbolism.

I am positive, secure and confident in myself: therefore, positive, secure, confident people are attracted to me everyday.

I know clearly who I am and what I want in personal relationships.

I attract powerfully positive and healthy people into my life.

I am caring, wise, supportive and fun to be with.

I feel completely at ease and comfortable with all people.

I am a winner in all my relationships.

I make valuable contributions in my relationships everyday.

I have a rich collection of friends who value my qualities.

I experience all my personal relationships with great consciousness.

I am always being guided in my personal relationships by a powerful and wise inner spiritual self.

I am powerfully and intuitively guided with any changes in my personal relationships.

Growth and change in my intimate love relationships is always directed toward good.

Affirmations For Relationships

Always take the time to write your affirmations with intention. Try to prepare yourself and your space while doing this. Meditate and visualize the kind of relationship you are seeking. Make sure your space is clean and fresh, then set your intention.

I am wise, honest, thoughtful, healthy in my love relationships, and others treat me the same.

I experience love deeply, and grow richer because of this everyday.

I am extremely successful in my love relationships.

I am a sensual, thoughtful, passionate lover, and my partner/s are sensual, thoughtful, and passionate in their love for me.

I am a fully alive human being with an ever-renewing trust for love in my life.

All my desires in relationships are being fulfilled everyday.

I possess complete ability to express my feelings, intentions, thoughts in all my relationships, and I express myself wisely.

Because I am completely confident in my health, honesty, and inner wisdom, I invest in personal relationships knowing deeply that I can deal with anything I may need to.

I know only love, and have completely forgotten how to be afraid in any of my relationships.

I always do the healthy thing in my relationships.

The Power Of Love

"Love - harmony, cooperation, and mutual assistance -
is the very foundation of my life.
In my every thought, emotion, and action
I express only Iove,
and this Divine Power makes everything right in my world."
Anonymous

This is such a beautiful quote that captures the quintessential essence of life. We always point out to our clients and students that without love in your life money, objects, career, etc. are simply meaningless. So, roll up your sleeves and take a long hard look at all your romance guas and see if you are inviting love into your life!

Affirmations For Health

You might be thinking why on earth are they giving me affirmations for my health in a book about love and relationships. Well, if we do not take control of our health, and choose to eat right, and exercise our body as well as our mind, then we lose any self confidence we might have had, let alone the ability to socialize and enjoy life to its fullest. Every gua or life station on the bagua relates to each other. Therefore, in order for you to attain a wonderful and loving relationship you must tend to your physical, emotional, and spiritual self.

Place any one of these affirmations in the middle third of the left wall of your bedroom from door entry. On the bagua this section represents our health as well as our self image. Take your time when choosing the affirmation, repeat to yourself often, and visualize yourself taking on these qualities. When placing the affirmation you can put it behind the proper imagery discussed in chapter one for this section of the bagua.

I have the power to control my health.

I am in control of my health and wellness.

I have abundant energy, vitality and well-being.

I am healthy in all aspects of my being.

I do not fear being unhealthy because I know that I control my own body.

I am filled with energy to do all the daily activities in my life.

My mind is at peace.

I love and care for my body and it cares for me.

Affirmations For Daily Living

I am at peace with the Universe.

I love and accept myself.

I am unique and loving, loved, and free.

I am safe and always feel protected.

I acknowledge all of my feelings because I am in touch with my feelings.

I am surrounded with loving, caring people in my life.

I am loving and accepting of others and this creates lasting friendships for me.

I trust my inner being to lead me in the right path.

I do all I can every day to make a loving environment for all those around me, including myself.

I am always connected with the Divine Love in the Universe.

My inner vision is always clear and focused.

We like these affirmations for our self image area of the bagua. Obviously a strong self image directly correlates with our ability to truly love another. Place as many of these affirmations along with the appropriate imagery discussed in chapter one, in the middle third of the left wall from door entry. As you may recall, we referred to this same section as our health. This particular life station on the bagua has dual representation.

Affirmations For Peace And Harmony In Your Life

I am at peace with myself.

I am always in harmony with the Universe.

I am filled with the Love of the Universal Divine Truth.

I am at peace with all those around me.

I have provided a harmonious place for myself and those I love.

The more honest I am with those around me, the more love is returned to me.

I express anger in appropriate ways so that peace and harmony are balanced at all times.

I am at one with the inner child in me.

Any one of these affirmations resonate well for our self image area. Place any or all of these affirmations in the middle third of the left wall from door entry. Once again, the importance of having a good self image has a profound impact in every area of our life. When we feel good about ourselves we are more willing to extend our hand to another. Properly addressing the self/health gua for a successful relationship is paramount. If you take a moment and refer to the Euro-Bagua you will see that section 1 (self/health) and section 7 (marriage/partnership) are directly opposite of each other. We call this a polarity, meaning one area is in cooperation with the other for harmony to exist.

In the end, positive affirmations combined with the power of intention and appropriate symbolism is an equation for success in whatever issue you are addressing. Feng Shui requires your ability to actively take part in the process of shifting the energy for a positive result to ensue.

4
Symbolism And Compass Direction

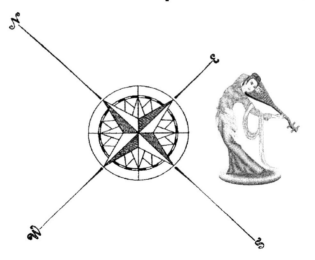

Symbolism

I once heard that Feng Shui was the science of metaphors and symbols. To a large extent this is true. We always tell our students that you can determine what issues your clients are having simply by the imagery and symbolism displayed throughout their space. In other words, the arrangement and choice of our possessions speaks volumes about what we are telling the Universe we want for ourselves. Therefore, our lives are either in direct harmony with the Universe or in opposition.

*E*very room in your space has a defining life station or experience identified by the bagua map. These life sections are also depicted on the land that contains the house or building. Since the intention of this book is to closely analyze the sections or guas that directly relate to relationships, we will evaluate the home from several perspectives. The architectural shape of the home, property, and individual rooms will play a vital role in determining the success of relationships in general. Obviously, we are going to assess the impact of appropriate imagery and symbolism in these guas as the power behind what we look at is immense.

*T*he first area to evaluate is the far right corner of the overall structure. This is the 5 (Leo) and 6 (Virgo) sections of the 12 parted Euro-Bagua. The Leo section is considered to be the heart of a room or building. If this area is missing, indented, or not addressed, the remaining guas tend to fall apart. We always tell our clients to make sure the right corner is working and is dynamic enough to make your heart sing. A good analogy from the physical body perspective is that no matter how good your other body organs function, if the heart doesn't work you're six feet under!

If the 5 (Leo) section is missing due to architectural shape, the chi or energy is also depleted here and therefore we know the occupants are lacking the fun and serendipitous quality in their relationship. The first thing to do is boost or elevate the chi to this section. We can do this in many ways. The easiest approach is to dig a hole approximately six inches deep at the intersecting point where the length and width of the house should meet to square off the structure. Place some sand in the hole and prop two terminating crystals with their points facing upward into the sand. Then fill over with remaining dirt and grass. Why two crystals? The right side of the bagua represents relationships and pairing qualities. These crystals are very powerful since they contain qualities of the Earth's vibration and therefore boost energy to this missing section.

This is the initial step to many other cures and remedies for this architectural issue. We can also place a bird feeder or lamp post at the same intersecting point to elevate the chi as well. If finances aren't an issue, then an addition, deck, patio, or landscaping can fill in this missing section and as a result boost the chi to the romance area of the bagua. You can then decorate this area with romantic statues, pink flowers, a bench for two, or whatever makes your heart sing!

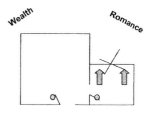

Now that we have addressed this problem externally we need to approach it internally. Go to the room that falls into the right corner of the structure. Place a mirror or romantic vista on the outside wall that abuts to the missing section. This will give the illusion of pushing this wall back and squaring off the shape of the building. You can also place terminating crystals on a shelf or the floor horizontally pointing towards this same outside wall to energetically shift the wall outward. A splash of mauve or pink and your on your way to bringing the fun back into your relationship.

Symbolic Imagery For The 5 Leo Section:

*I*f you remember from the Euro-bagua, the 5 (Leo) section falls in the far right corner of any space. The interesting thing here is the human eye always gravitates to the right upon entering a room. Therefore, it behooves us to place a powerful image to act as a focal point for the room. This image can be romantic or fun to fulfill the energy that naturally resonates to this area. Some examples might be:

- Field of sunflowers
- Roses
- Romantic scene
- Two round or heart shaped pillows on a love seat
- Two rose quartz crystals
- Fresh flowers (red or pink)
- Heart shaped faceted crystal
- Love knot

*Y*ou may also address this area with anything that you and your partner enjoy doing together. This is a very fun, creative and spontaneous area - so go ahead and be a little adventuresome.

*O*nce you have taken care of the glaring issue like architecture, then you can focus on the individual rooms and address the guas appropriately. Remember, any missing section can be dealt with the same way but then the colors and imagery would need to conform to the missing gua in question.

The most important room to address for relationships is the bedroom. If you take a look at your bedroom and superimpose the bagua via door entry you can evaluate several sections that bind the relationship. Although it's nice to have fun, we also need other qualities to enfold our relationship and keep it strong. Before we can consider being in an unconditional loving partnership we must make sure we have fully accepted who we are. If we do not respect and love thyself, then we will never find a soulful love with another. And where do you think we analyze our space for self image? You guessed it; the Aries or 1 sector of the Euro-Bagua.

In addition to this sector representing our health it also resonates to how we view oneself. Therefore, the key is to place a strong image of how we ultimately see ourselves, not how we think other people want to see us. For example, if you see your highest self being a Goddess, then place a statue or piece of art depicting just that! Take it one step further, write an affirmation about your self image and tuck it in a drawer, behind the piece of artwork, or statue. The process of writing an affirmation brings a thought into reality. After all, never underestimate the power of intention.

If there is a window in this gua of your bedroom, you can still address this section by placing a figurine statue on the sill, or hanging a red tassel or crystal in the window to boost the chi and pick up on the red color that resonates to this section.

Another area we can evaluate in the bedroom for relationships is the Gemini or 3 section. This is the left corner of the room specifically the far left 1/3rd of the back wall. Although this is part of the wealth section, it also represents how we communicate with others. It is a rather playful and yang area, so that is just what we need to do here; yang it up! Since Mercury is the ruling planet, it craves reflective, metallic, or communication devices. Therefore, this is a perfect place for your telephone or perhaps a battery operated metal clock. A small mirror will also find itself right at home in this section. Just make sure it does not reflect the door entrance of the room because all that wonderful chi will bounce out before it has a chance to circulate throughout the space. Also, be mindful in placing the mirror so it does not reflect your body when you are in bed, otherwise a restless sleep will be the result.

The 5 or Leo section is another area to address within the bedroom. This section is the far right 1/3rd of the back wall. This is the area that represents the spontaneity in relationships. Dress it up with pictures of you and your significant other having fun on vacation if you are already in a relationship. If you are looking to attract another person into your life, then place romantic imagery or pairs of things showing the universe you are ready to share your life with another.

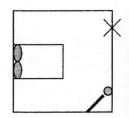

Let's move next door to the far 1/3rd of the right wall and take a look at the Virgo 6 section. From the romantic perspective this section deals with the engagement period. In other words, the Leo section is where you flip off your shoes and have a blast, and the Virgo section is where the convincing goes on. We mean you're the one! If we examine this gua from a romantic perspective, suitable imagery would include musical instruments in the form of artwork, a sculpture, or the actual instrument itself. You may also choose to display a miniature collection of instruments on a shelf or shadow box. The Virgo energy that resides here just loves attention to detail that a collection evokes.

With this next section the true commitment occurs. The Libra 7 section, middle 1/3rd of the right wall is the polarity of the Aries 1 section. The premise of this gua is optimism, where one is ready to extend thy hand and share with another. This section represents the legalities behind a committed partnership. In this gua we want to see the formal marriage photos, romantic themes or pairing qualities. If you are not married but are looking to do so, you can place two roses with a Peridot stone and write down the qualities you are looking for in a mate. Place it in this gua at the present level, or middle 1/3rd of the wall height, and see who comes into your life.

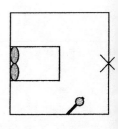

This next section can be very secretive yet sensual. The Scorpio 8 section is the near 1/3ʳᵈ of the right wall. Many times it falls behind a door and may not have the space to be addressed. That's okay since this area takes on desert-like qualities, but go ahead and place a garnet stone there if that's all you have room for. However, if you do have the space, then think sensual imagery like Georgia O'Keefe's sensual flowers or a statue of two lovers embracing.

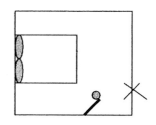

If all you seem to do is attract immature lovers then you need to inject a little mature energy into the space. You can achieve this by placing a romantic image or pair of objects, nothing childlike, in the Capricorn or 10 section. This gua resonates with the father and responsibility. If there happens to be a door located in this section you can place two rose quartz stones above the door jam and a romantic doorknob chime on the door. Every time your partner passes through the doorway a responsible mature energy will generate within the space.

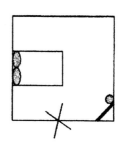

Finally, place an unusual object or abstract piece of art in the Aquarius 11 section to attract new people into your life. This section is located in the far 1/3rd of the front wall to the room and is the polarity to the 5 Leo section. In order to have fun dating you need to network and meet people!

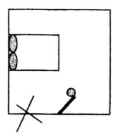

You can also encourage a socializing atmosphere by letting in natural southern sunlight. If your home does not have many windows in this direction, make sure you have bright full spectrum lighting here. You can also decorate with brighter yang colors if your shy and need to promote outgoing behavior in yourself.

Equality

Once you evaluate and address the guas pertaining to relationships in your bedroom, take a look at how your bed is positioned in the room. Is it situated on the center of the wall with equal distance on either side?

Do you have identical nightstands in height and width on either side of the bed? If you have a lamp on the nightstand, is it identical to the lamp on the other nightstand? What I'm trying to get at here is equality in the relationship. If you only have one nightstand, or if they are unequal in size, then the person with the higher piece of furniture is controlling the relationship. Likewise, if the bed is positioned where one person must squeeze in between a wall to have access to their side of the bed, or even worse yet, have to climb over the other person to enter the bed, then that person is being controlled or squeezed in the relationship. The underlying premise here is to position the bed and furniture so there is equality when you look into the room.

Does The Room Nurture You?

The bedroom should elicit a feeling of comfort, a sense of being enfolded and protected. For this reason the room should be decorated on the yin side. You want to avoid harsh yang materials like Formica or Lacquer furniture. These materials are too harsh and the synthetic components outgas causing potential health problems. Wood furniture is soothing, yet provides us with the structure and support our bodies need. When choosing linens strive for 100% cotton to eliminate static charge to the body; however, you can be a bit daring and indulge yourself with the romantic feel of silk or chenille fabric.

Colors

Aim for romantic or nurturing colors when it comes to the bedroom, as the purpose for this room is relaxation and intimacy. Colors like mauve, burgundy, green, plum, or skin tone are all good choices. Remember to pick up the romance colors in the bed linens and accessories too, especially if you do not choose to place color on the walls.

Avoid colors like blue, lavender and yellow for the bedroom. These colors are inappropriate for many reasons. Blue is a cool color and will make it difficult for the couple to be passionate. Lavender is a very chaste energy and obviously totally inappropriate for the master bedroom. Yellow is the color of intellect and therefore too thought provoking for such a room. It works much better for an office or study. Furthermore, yellow activates the respiratory system and could incite colds and bronchial conditions.

Lighting

Steer clear of halogen, fluorescent or spot lighting in the bedroom. Not only does this type of lighting cause negative physiological effects, but it is way too bright for the purpose of the room. Think soft, low lighting, or candle lighting for the bedroom to enhance relaxation and intimacy.

Compass Direction

In addition to addressing the relationship guas from the three door entry, we may also address the guas from a directional energy. By addressing the guas from a compass perspective, we are opening up the energies on an emotional level. If we take the Euro-Bagua and note the compass direction for the guas, we can then place appropriate imagery in those relationship directions. The easiest way to do this is to stand in the middle of the room you are addressing and hold a compass waist height. Make sure you do not have any jewelry on or anything metal, as it will alter the compass reading. Find the compass direction that relates to the gua you want to address and go ahead and place the appropriate symbol there. The impact is tremendous when you work with both the three door and compass system.

Aries Section 1

The compass direction that represents this gua is 90 degrees due east. The east direction is very ambitious, enthusiastic and confident. We can enhance this direction in two ways. First, we might place an image that represents how we see ourselves ultimately. We may also draw upon those positive qualities by placing a very healthy plant or wood element in this direction. This is a sure way to boost self confidence, health and overall vitality. Not bad qualities to have when looking for that special someone.

Gemini Section 3

This gua is 150 degrees SSE. It is a direction that is very persistent, creative and communicative. If you want to enhance your communication skills, then place reflective or metallic objects in this direction following the energy that resonates from the Gemini section of the Euro-Bagua. If you want to be more creative, then place a plant or wood element in this direction. In the Eastern practice the southeast relates to the wood element.

Leo Section 5

This romantically fun section aligns with 210 degrees on the compass. The southwest is a very practical, realistic, caring and intimate direction. If you want to capitalize on these qualities while injecting some fun romance into your life, then place romantic imagery here along with some earth elements in the form of crystals, stones, ceramic or terracotta.

Virgo Section 6

This gua aligns to 240 degrees WSW. It is considered to be the engagement period, the final stage before the major plunge into marriage. Romantic images, a pair of love birds, or a musical instrument can be placed in this direction to enhance the devotional energy you have towards your future life partner.

Libra Section 7

The Libra 7 section is all about the committed partnership. It is the legal formality that goes with the territory of marriage, or for that matter, any partnership. To capture this energy on an emotional level place romantic themes, pairs of objects or qualities you want in your life partner at 270 degrees due west. Contentment, pleasure and relaxation are also some qualities that spew from this direction. To enhance these qualities within your life, place any type of metal element here since metal is the element for the west direction.

Scorpio Section 8

The sensuality that seeps out of this gua acts as a flame for any relationship. Scorpio aligns with 300 degrees WNW on the compass. To draw upon this energetic quality emotionally, simply place a sensual image on that directional line. The northwestern direction also is associated with self discipline and organization. To enhance these qualities within yourself, place a metal element in this direction of your home. This can be metal itself or anything oval, round, white or any of the metal colors.

Capricorn Section 10

*H*aving a responsible mature relationship is reassuring. To align those energies in your space, place a photo of you and your significant other at 360 degrees in a room you spend a great deal of time in. By doing this, you align your own auric pattern with that of the responsible energy that directional gua emits. If it is your partner that lacks responsibility and self discipline, then place a metal element in the northwest sector of your entire home or in their favorite room.

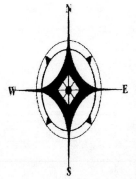

*T*he north direction also represents a peaceful, quiet energy that also evokes independence and flexibility according to directional theory. If you need to enhance qualities such as those within yourself, then place a water element, perhaps a fountain in this direction of your overall home, but not if it falls in your wealth section because money drains our wealth in our Western culture.

Aquarius Section 11

*T*o further enhance your social skills, address 30 degrees NNE compass direction with anything outrageously outlandish! This is especially important if you are shy about meeting new people. You can also decorate your space more yang to boost your ability to be a bit more outgoing, or enhance the south direction of your home with fire elements like candles, red colors or pointed shapes.

*T*he northeast direction has a motivational, decisive energy to it which are excellent attributes to have. Capitalize on these directional qualities by placing an earth element in this direction of your overall home in the form of crystals, stones, ceramic, terracotta or colors like orange, yellow or brown.

Center Of Home

The center of your home relates to powerful, forceful and attention-seeking qualities. Obviously, these are not very attractive characteristics to have. Therefore, it behooves you to tone these energetic qualities down. We can achieve this by simply uprooting the representing earth element here by placing a wood element in the center position of your home. This should only be done if you possess these strong behavioral qualities and believe it is a deterrent for you when meeting people. The center of the bagua also represents overall health and stability, so the earth element is important in this location.

Unrealistic Romantic Expectations

We are all guilty of conjuring up the ideal lover. However, if you find yourself being overly picky and perhaps ignoring a potential good partner, then you need to expose yourself to some southeastern and western energy. The southeast relates to the spring season and morning hours. Because of this, it generates a refreshing outlook on issues that may have been bogging you down. The western energy is one of contentment and acceptance. If you place a healthy plant and a daily fresh bowl of water in the southeast, you can generate these qualities into your life. Likewise, if you place a metal object with red accents in the western part of your home, you will activate the energy from this direction and find contentment in what you have.

Mundane Sex

After awhile any relationship sexually can become mundane or nonexistent. Besides addressing all the relationship guas with appropriate imagery, you need to call upon compass directional support. Activate the chi energy of the west and the north. These directions relate to sexual energy. You can simply do this by positioning your head on these directional walls. You can also activate sexual energy by using the colors purple, red, pink or cream. Make sure the bedroom is comfortable and clutter free, and does not have any distracting components like TV's, books or computers. A vase filled with fresh flowers and a few candles will also encourage sexual activity.

If you find your partner is boring sexually, you can inject more yang components into the bedroom through metal, stone and glass elements. You can also make sure your lovers diet contains more yang foods like seafood, root vegetables and grains.

Romance Tips For The Bedroom

Whether you are in a relationship, looking for one, or just need to kick it up a notch, the *Romantic Bedroom Checklist* can put you on the right path. We suggest you take a notebook or journal and write down those areas in your bedroom that do not meet the guidelines of the checklist below.

• Remove all clutter especially in any romance guas.

• Discard any old love letters or gifts from previous relationships. This includes the bed! If that is not possible then replace the linens and mattress or smudge it with essential oils or sage.

• Remove any family photos. We do not want mom, dad, the in-laws, our children, pets or friends viewing our intimate space!

• Use romantic or nurturing colors in the bedding, accessories or walls of the room. The colors include mauve, burgundy, plum, green or skin tone.

• Remember to position your bed in a command position with equality in mind. This includes equal height and width in nightstands and fixtures too.

• When it comes to artwork think romance, romance, romance.

• No religious icons in the relationship guas. Keep them to the spiritual area only.

• Spritz sheets and room with pure essential romance oils like Jasmine, Pink Grapefruit or Ylang Ylang.

• Utilize low lighting and candles to encourage relaxation and romance.

• Incorporate natural materials to minimize potential health issues.

• Avoid TV's, clock radios, computers or anything that emits electromagnetic frequencies in this room to ensure healthful sleep.

• Avoid desks, work material or workout equipment, as the focus should be on your partner.

• Leave the water fountains out or you will be running to the bathroom all night long.

• Make sure the head of the bed does not share the wall where the toilet is placed or in the morning you will feel drained. In addition, the door to an adjoining bathroom should remain closed as well as the toilet lid.

• Window treatment should cover the entire window and block out any light pollution.

• One plant is enough for the bedroom. Make sure it is no taller than 3 feet in height and positioned no closer than 6 feet to the bed.

Maximize The Outcome

When addressing the relationship guas to enhance or attract a new love, always begin the cures in the bedroom. Once you have successfully addressed your bedroom, you can slowly approach the other rooms within your home. Begin with rooms you spend the most time in, then proceed to those rooms you spend the least amount of time in. As you address each gua, set an intention for what you are doing. You may also write an actual affirmation and place it in a drawer within the gua, or behind the artwork or symbol you are placing for the cure. Once you have completed your indoor space, proceed to the yard and address the relevant guas. Take your time, keep a journal and try to place one cure at a time so if something goes wrong you know exactly what you did.

5
Colors, Crystals
&
Romantic Lighting

Colors

Color is nourishment to our soul and plays a very important role in Feng Shui. Our personal, spiritual and cultural associations affect our experience of color. For instance, our Western culture likes the planets Venus, the planet of love and Jupiter the planet of expansion. Venus because we love to shower ourselves in beautiful things, and Jupiter because we always want more. From the sky these planets give off a beautiful bluish hue. Blue being America's favorite color. Saturn, the planet of structure, happens to be the favorite planet of the East and the color that comes off this planet is yellow. Yes, this happens to be China's favorite color. You can see how colors are associated with our origin.

Our body needs to be around color. It helps us to balance and improve our body's energy centers known as our chakras. Color enhances our moods for relaxation, health, inspiration and protection.

Every color has a symbolic meaning and effects chi energy differently, so it is important to be careful where we use our colors. Since we are addressing the bedroom in this book, the colors we recommend will be for romance and relaxation.

White is devoid of color and being around white all the time can be unhealthy, not to mention the sterile feeling it gives you. Keep white walls out of the bedroom if at all possible. Restrictions with some condo associations or landlords sometimes prohibit any other color except white on the walls. If that's the case, then be sure to add some romantic colors such as the reds, pinks, greens, and soothing earth tones to the room in your wallpaper patterns, bed linens, comforters or duvets, area rugs, pillows, pictures, etc.

You will read in many Feng Shui books that red, white and pink are love colors. Take the color red for instance. Red is about romance but has been known to stimulate the senses and raise the blood pressure. It also has the characteristics of the fire element in five element theory. You know the expression "I was so angry I could see red"! Even though some colors are considered auspicious and romantic, red being a love color would not be the romantic color to paint the bedroom. Things could get very heated and we mean in an angry way not a sexual way. Accents are the way to go with this color.

Romantic Colors

According to the principles of Feng Shui, the colors pink, red and white are associated with romance. These colors evoke romantic feelings between two people and create a sensual background for romance.

The color pink is associated with pleasure, so using this color brings out your playfulness and feelings of romance. Think of cupid and valentines day, the holiday of love and flirtation.

Red stimulates the senses and is associated with passion and excitement, but if we over do it, red can make us argumentative and lead to bickering. It is best not to use a red bedspread, as red can ignite anger. Be sure not to overwhelm your room with too much of one color. Keep it balanced.

Think about adding touches of reds, pinks or even burgundy in your sheets, throw pillows, candles, flowers and other decorative details.

A slender vase with long stemmed red roses embodies the mood for romance. Place them in the romance area of the bedroom-your far right hand corner of your room from the door entrance.

As with everything, when applying Feng Shui, one of the first things to be aware of is making sure your environment is clutter free. Release your mind, and allow yourself to be in a total love mode!

Colors

Blue is the opposite of red, and although known as another love color, it is more of the devotional love a mother has for her child or children. We recommend you leave this color choice for a child's bedroom. We don't think as adults we want to be devotional to our spouse in the bedroom. Another place for blue is the kitchen because it is a cool and calming color so it curbs the appetite. If you find yourself munching a little too much, think about purchasing some blue pots.

Stay away from the color peach. In Feng Shui this choice of color in the bedroom has been known to stir up infidelity and extra marital affairs. Yellow is another color we don't suggest using in the bedroom. Yellow is about intellect and contemplative energies, obviously qualities we don't need in the bedroom. These type of qualities are better off in an office environment. In addition, too much of this color can aid in respiratory problems; another reason we don't like it in the bedroom.

Violet is a color that isn't recommended in an adult bedroom either. While the colors violet and purple are often associated with spiritualism, when mixed with white it creates a color representing chastity; lavender. Chastity doesn't equate to sex. Now on the other hand, If you have a teenage daughter this would be a good color choice for her room. Remember the representation though. If you want her to go off and get married eventually, change the bedroom colors to pinks, burgundies, greens and soothing earth tones once she is older.

Crystals

Crystals fill a home with positive energy. They add light and color to any room you use them in. They not only generate great energy but also deflect negative energies. Each stone and crystal emits subtle vibrations that influence a specific area of our body. Our body is made of the same elements found in stones and crystals, so matching the stone or crystal to its specific use allows us to get the most benefit from these natural gifts of harmony. This gives each one a unique vibration rate and quality.

More importantly, since we are talking about romance in Feng Shui, Mother Earth gives us a number of crystals that are especially tuned to direct energy to assist people in the realm of love and its related problems.

If you are in between relationships and wish to attract that perfect someone, then you need the moonstone. This stone is known to attract a soul mate. Moonstone possesses a great number of spiritual and healing properties. For men, it can help them reach out to their creative and emotional side, which we know most men repress and most women what to see more of in their significant other.

Moonstone: Comes in different colors and brings great balance to life, balancing yin and yang. It is extremely good for soothing stresses and anxieties that are brought about at different times in our hectic life.

Nephrite Jade: Works with the heart chakra, so this stone resonates well with Rose Quartz to promote giving and acceptance of love. It enables the holder to open their heart and receive new energies making them more aware of their strengths, and how to use them in new ways.

Hematite: This stone is silver in color and will help you maintain unconditional love in your heart. It resonates to the root chakra that keeps us balanced and centered.

Crystals

*I*n Feng Shui, a rose quartz crystal is very powerful and is referred to as the love stone. It creates and enhances harmony. To help keep the love you have and make it grow stronger, place a pair of rose quartz crystals in your relationship area. It channels love energy and works with the heart chakra by enhancing emotions. It has the ability to soothe and nurture your emotions while bringing an unlimited perspective of love into a relationship. Any fears of using your heart or showing others your love are alleviated with this romantic stone.

*Y*our southwest direction and far right corner are the two powerful romance areas to enhance. With a compass, stand in the center of your bedroom and locate the southwest direction. Display the rose quartz as a pair in this direction to give balance & harmony. They are a beautiful stone in a rough form or tumbled (smooth), and come polished in heart shape.

*H*aving things in pairs in the relationship area symbolically represents love, unity and romance. Whether you are enhancing a relationship or trying to build one, placing just one crystal would be counterproductive. You are telling the universe there is no room for romance. Be sure to place two rose quartz or two pink faceted crystals in the far right hand corner of your bedroom.

*O*ther pink crystals for your romance area are the Inesite (rare pink crystal) pink aventurine, pink tourmaline, pink sapphire, pink agate or pink calcite.

Cleansing Your Crystals/Stones

*B*efore you start to use your crystals you should cleanse them.

*S*ince crystals hold your energies and help in removing or changing energy, achieving balance, etc, you want to cleanse them routinely. You don't want the stored negative energy they removed from you or your significant other to remain in the crystals. Below are some ways your can cleanse your crystals.

Smudging: *H*old your crystal or crystals over the smoke of incense for a few minutes to smudge the gem or crystal and clear the energy inside. You can also use a sage stick.

Soaking: *S*ea salt dissolved in warm spring water is another great way to cleanse your stones. Never use a metal bowl, you should always use glass or ceramic one. Let them soak for approximately 4-6 hours. Rinse them in cool water when you are finished to remove any salt. Do not re-use this salt water because the negative energies you just removed from your crystals are now in the water. Avoid salt water soaking with stones like opal, lapis, or any other porous stones.

Running Water: *P*lace your stones in a mesh bag and immerse them in an out door stream or lake for a few hours. This both cleanses **AND** re-energizes your stones.

Sunlight: *P*lace your gemstone or crystal in warm sunlight for 4 hours.

Moonlight: *P*lace your gemstones or crystals in direct moonlight overnight. You can place them on your windowsill, if you have the room.

Romantic Lighting

Romance is all about you feeling close with someone, as well as bringing your chi energy to merge with a significant other in a harmonious way. You can create the stage in your bedroom using certain lighting. Soft lighting in this room creates a romantic atmosphere.

Avoid using direct lighting and glaring bulbs. Try using lighting such as sconces with low watt incandescent light bulbs, which can be reflected off a wall or ceiling. The silhouette on the wall can create a romantic image.

Help stimulate the loving energy and create the intimate atmosphere that you wish to provide for your space by lighting candles. You can group them in pairs or in heart shape dishes with crystals to represent the relationship, and at the same time evoke the romantic background for your bedroom.

Another form of light that is romantic because of its soothing glow, is a salt lamp or salt light tea holder. When heated with a bulb or candle flame, it cleanses the air of any unhealthy positive ions.

Give yourself and your significant other, time and energy to find your own
level of harmony and romance, and let the magic begin.

6

Essential Oils & Scents

Essential Oils

Aromatherapy is the practice of using volatile plant oils for psychological and physical well-being. It is recommended to purchase aromatherapy oils that are pure and natural. Products that contain artificial ingredients will give you little benefit, mask the true aroma that the essence provides, and may make you sensitive to the oil.

Feng Shui is about nature and our environment. Using the elements Mother Earth provides us with such as essential oils, help to bring clarity and appreciation to our lives making us the most productive we can be. Besides crystals, natural essential oils are tools we recommend in Feng Shui to stimulate or enhance our lives. They are known to be electrical, refreshing and raise the energy vibration wherever they are used. Oils affect us emotionally, mentally, physically and spiritually.

We work with **Nature's Sunshine Products** because of their high quality. Using essential oils strengthens your ability to recognize the influences obstructing you from achieving joy and harmony. We recommend spraying aromatherapy oils or using a diffuser to help maintain a field of energy while stimulating areas of your life.

To enhance your love life and activate a romantic mood, start by misting any of these pure essential oils in the *(romance/relationship)* areas. Give romance a double boost and spray the far right corner of your bedroom, and if it doesn't fall in the southwest direction, then find it with your compass and spray that area as well with any of these scents. Rose Bulgaria, Pink Grapefruit, Ylang Ylang, Lavender, Lemon or Patchouli which is known to be an aphrodisiac.

Essential Oils

In Feng Shui the bedroom is one of the most important rooms in our home and has the most affect on us when it comes to our health and wellness. The bedroom is also one of the rooms where we should be romantic. When our bodies are well rested we function better, are more productive, energetic, healthier, alert, and ultimately have more energy to find the time to be romantic with our partners.

When essential oils are diffused it increases the oxygen, fills the air with a fresh aromatic scent, and increases negative ions in the house which inhibits bacterial growth. There are several scents that we recommend you use, but suggest you try each scent and see which one works for you. Even when a scent resonates to a particular area of the bagua, only use it if you like the scent. Smell is one of the most powerful senses we possess, so if you activate your romance area with an essential oil that is offensive to you, there will be a lot of negative chi in the air and not enough romance.

Essential Oils

*E*ssential oils can:

- **Purify** by removing metallic particles and toxins from the air.
- **Increase** atmospheric oxygen.
- **Increase** ozone and negative ions in the house, which inhibits bacterial growth.
- **Fill** the air with a fresh, herbal aromatic scent.

*H*ere are some of the essential oils we recommend and their therapeutic qualities.

Grapefruit lifts depression and aids in cases of nervous exhaustion and stress.

Helchrysum soothes your body and raises your spirits with the subtle scent of honey and flora. It heals physical and emotional scarring and opens the heart.

Lavender can be used to alleviate anxiety, stress and tension, by claming, soothing and relaxing the body and mind. Unlike most essential oils, lavender is very gentle and does not need to be diluted before using it on the body. A few drops on a pillow or your sheets can calm you and allow for a peaceful rest.

Rose Bulgaria is calming and can help you unwind and relax. It is used in most romantic bath blends because of its aphrodisiac properties. It is also used for healing, balancing, romance and pleasure.

Ylang Ylang can be helpful with anxiety, physical exhaustion, impotence, insomnia, depression and stress.

Scents

Like color and crystals, scents play a part in our emotions, and thought processes. Incense are classified as an herb that is used for religious, medicinal and relaxation purposes. They are wonderful for coping or aiding rest and relaxation after a hectic day, or to prepare the mind for meditation. Its aroma-therapeutic qualities have been found to provide soothing natural relief from the symptoms of insomnia. We mention insomnia because it is a big factor of breakups in relationships. The act of burning incense raises vibrational rates and relaxes the senses.

Some incenses can be overpowering, so just like essential oils, it is recommended to try some out before you purchase that special scent. Opening your windows and letting the fresh air in is also a good idea when burning your incense.

For your convenience we have included the Euro-Bagua with essential oils that naturally resonate to each gua or life station. This was developed by our Feng Shui masters and is a wonderful way to boost a particular area of your life. Obviously you want to hone in on any of the scents that fall into the relationship guas (5, 6, 7 & 8) to add a little spice to your love life!

Essential Oils For The Guas

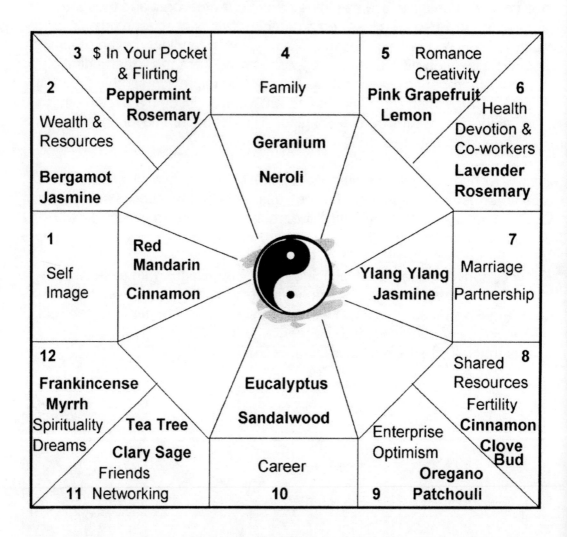

2 Wealth & Resources **Bergamot Jasmine**	**3** $ In Your Pocket & Flirting **Peppermint Rosemary**	**4** Family **Geranium Neroli**	**5** Romance Creativity **Pink Grapefruit Lemon**	**6** Health Devotion & Co-workers **Lavender Rosemary**

2 Wealth & Resources **Bergamot Jasmine**

3 $ In Your Pocket & Flirting **Peppermint Rosemary**

4 Family

5 Romance Creativity **Pink Grapefruit Lemon**

6 Health Devotion & Co-workers **Lavender Rosemary**

Geranium Neroli

1 Self Image

Red Mandarin Cinnamon

Ylang Ylang Jasmine

7 Marriage Partnership

12 **Frankincense Myrrh** Spirituality Dreams

Tea Tree Clary Sage Friends **11** Networking

Eucalyptus Sandalwood Career **10**

Enterprise Optimism **Oregano Patchouli** **9**

8 Shared Resources Fertility **Cinnamon Clove Bud**

Euro-Bagua Copyright by: Drs. Ralph & Lahni DeAmicis

Pampering Yourself

When the chaotic world is draining you, sometimes the best thing you can do is take a few minutes out for a breather. Everyone needs a treat, so unwind and de-stress from your daily routine by using pure aromatherapy oils. This is a great way to relax, refocus yourself, and Increase your energy level towards the road to a healthy lifestyle. All essential oils, except Lavender, are concentrated and should be mixed with a carrier oil so as not to irritate the skin.

Massages: Massaging with essential oils is the most efficient method to release tension. The oils are absorbed and can be heated into the skin promoting a feeling of relaxation and well being.

Bath: Pamper yourself by adding 4-6 drops of some relaxing essential oils to your bath water such as Sandalwood, Lavender, Chamomile, Cleary Sage and Ylang Ylang.

To begin your day feeling rejuvenated, add to your bath water some Myrrh or any of the citrus fragrances such as Grapefruit, Lemon, or Lime. Citrus oils should be added carefully so as not to irritate the skin. Do not exceed 3 drops. Enjoy yourself-after all you deserve it!

7
Feng Shui Your Landscape For Love

Feng Shui Your Landscape For Love

Applying Feng Shui to the yard through small adjustments of pathways, materials, flowerbeds, birdbaths and statues can make a substantial difference on how the chi feels and flows. It also will prepare the chi to enter the front door or mouth of your home. Obviously, we want sheng chi (good energy) to imbue our space, and in order to do that we must first address it from the outside property.

Just as the overall shape of a building can be irregular and therefore have guas missing, the yard too can be irregular shaped. The difference is, if the gua is missing on the property but not the house, that related aspect of your life is being kept quiet. In other words, the yard represents our public life whereas the house represents our personal life. To put it more bluntly, if your property is missing the right corner or relationship gua and the house is not, it is possible one of the occupants is having an affair and keeping it very quiet.

The key to working with an odd shaped yard is to be able to create boundaries that flow gracefully into another section. You can accomplish this through curving pathways, shrubbery, climbers, borders, fences, stones, lighting, sound, and life force energy. All of these components will activate a balanced chi and help modulate it to all areas of the yard including overly yin or shaded areas.

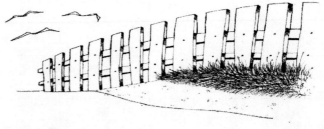

Just as we addressed the romance guas from the interior, we can do the same on the exterior property and show the universe from a social perspective what we desire in life.

One aspect of the 1-Aries section relates to our self-image and therefore should show strength to support the polarity of the 7-Libra gua or partnership section. Planting a strong tree or evergreen will effectively root this area and keep the self-esteem intact. Adding some red flowers or a statue of a human image you resonate with are additional symbols appropriate for this gua. This section falls on the middle third of the left side of the property utilizing the three gate entry or 90 degrees due east using the compass theory. Since the position of this gua may present with limited space, it behooves you to be flexible with your landscape design.

1-Aries ⟶

We all know how important it is to communicate socially and personally. A great way to address the 3-Gemini section of the property (far left hand corner or 150 degrees south-by-southeast), is to place a gazing ball in a gold or silver color in this section. Not only will it brighten up a potentially shaded area, but it can reflect the sun or a water element from across the way while satisfying the playful yang component of this gua. Other objects such as metal chimes or a weathervane will also aid in communicating with others on a social level. The key is to create movement here while using reflective or metallic materials. Be creative and have fun with this section as Gemini is very childlike.

3 -Gemini

If we want to create a romantic garden that will attract lovers, we must activate the chi energy of the southwest and west and work with romantic imagery and colors. There are a few ways to accomplish this depending on the particular focus for the individual. If you are looking for a romantic retreat, you could plant several flowerbeds along with bushes that are tall enough to create a private space. Inside this space you could place a bench for two or a small bistro dining table. Several lantern lights and candles with a water feature, and you have a hideaway oasis in your backyard.

You can create this romantic garden either on the right side of the yard or in the southwestern direction. The first position is applying the bagua to the overall property with the house in the center and using the three gate entry where the openings are located to the front of the property. The second position is using the compass school method and finding the southwest sector of the yard and creating the garden there.

Another way to address the relationship area of the yard is to create an area for activities that you and your partner enjoy to share. For example, if you enjoy gardening then plant a vegetable or flower garden in the 5-Leo and 6-Virgo section where the two of you can tend to the garden together. If you are single, then landscape this area with pairs of pink flowers, two decorative stones, or plant an apple tree that bares fruit signifying growth for relationships. Make sure this area remains weeded and not overgrown, as it will indicate to the universe you are committed to tending to your relationships.

In addition to addressing the right corner (5-Leo, 6-Virgo guas), you can also tend to the 7-Libra section. This area from the three door entry will fall on the right middle third side of the property. Many times the side of the property is not a big area and therefore design is more restricted. You can still capture the essence of romance with proper colored flowers, statues and chimes that have a flare of romance to them.

→ **7-Libra**

We can also address the 8-Scorpio section of the property or helpful people sector. A beautiful sensual statue of two lovers embracing bordered with deep burgundy flowers, makes a perfect statement socially of the kind of romance you look for in a relationship. Once again you may have to be flexible here with your landscape design, as this section falls to the right front side of the property.

If you want to call helpful people into you life to assist you in finding the right person or perhaps council a problematic relationship, then take out your compass and find the northwest sector and place a weathervane there. The constant movement will generate chi to this section and call people to you.

→ **8 -Scorpio**

You can also liven up the 11-Aquarius section of the yard by placing unusual lawn art, or an array of colored flowers to increase your exposure to other people. This is especially helpful if you are somewhat shy and need a little push to socialize and meet new people. Again, you may have to be flexible here since it is the far left front of the property and in direct view for all to see.

11-Aquarius ⟶

Feng Shui Landscaping Tips

Most people believe Feng Shui principles apply to the internal space or building; however, what we need to remember is Feng Shui originated in the outside environment. Be that as it may, it behooves us to incorporate these principles from the outside in. Below are some main factors to employ while incorporating yard Feng Shui.

- Make your face to the world, or better known in Feng Shui as your front yard, very auspicious. The idea is to take people's breath away every time they pass by.

- Add features that create sound and movement such as chimes, bird feeders, or fountains to appeal to our senses while stimulating the stagnate chi.

- Always trim back foliage so it doesn't conflict with pathways or the building structure.

- Use varying heights of landscaping to achieve a smooth transition from one area level to another.

- Choose plants, bushes, and flowers according to the soil type and climate. In other words, when one plant dies off another variation should replace it.

- Use curved pathways with varying materials such as slate, brick, stone, or wood chips; it not only adds drama, but helps modulate the chi.

- Install adequate lighting as chi flows poorly in any area that is too dark.

- Add a water feature of either a pond, pool, or fountain to stimulate and cultivate chi.

- Choose plants with a variety of textures, smells, and colors to stimulate the senses and rejuvenate sluggish chi.

- Keep an open area, preferable in the center of the yard, and place a large stone or statue to stabilize the property.

- Choose a romantic statue for a relationship gua like two lovers embracing or Venus "The Goddess of Love" to symbolize how you want your love life to be.

- Let roses or scented jasmine climbers grow over a trellis and waft a romantic scent while providing privacy to a secret garden.

- Design an area of stillness to relax or meditate in. Use large rocks as a stabilizer, bamboo chimes to quiet the senses, and koi fish to create movement.

- Plant trees and plants that move easily in the slightest breeze, such as an Aspen tree along with other movement generating objects like chimes, flags, weathervanes, and wind socks. Movement is essential to keep chi healthy and circulate throughout every gua.

The dynamics of landscape Feng Shui are immense and address our lives from the social aspect. It allows you to paint the incoming chi with auspicious symbols and imagery that ultimately project your life desires. So roll up your sleeves and get your hands into "Mother Earth" and create the garden of your dreams.

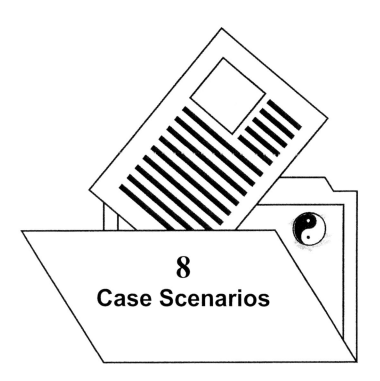

8
Case Scenarios

Case Scenarios

If you are wondering if anything will actually change in your life after incorporating the principles of Feng Shui within your space, then forge ahead and meet those who have adjusted and reaped the rewards.

In this chapter you will read about various clients who experienced life altering changes after incorporating the principles of this age old art and science within their lives. We are truly grateful to those who were ready to acknowledge the laws of nature and welcome Feng Shui into their homes and as a result their lives.

Meet client **A**: a middle age attractive single female looking to improve her love life. When she contacted us she expressed her frustration about the "dating scene". She had no difficulty meeting men, yet it baffled her as to why no one would pursue a relationship with her. After taking a thorough history on this client, we learned she had been divorced for ten years and was definitely ready to have a serious commitment in her life. The architectural shape of her floor plans were intact in terms of the overall shape; however, the attached garage was located in the overall 7-Libra sector, the area of commitment in the Euro-Bagua. A garage is not a living space and therefore lacks the stability of a room. Did you catch that? It lacks stability!

When we arrived for her onsite consultation, we noticed every room in her townhouse contained imagery of horses and an odd number of women. Many of her relationship guas also contained this imagery or were not addressed at all. It was very obvious to us as to why men were not pursuing a relationship with her. Her walls were screaming out to the universe, "I'm committed to my horses and being alone"!

When we entered her bedroom we noticed several things. First, she had a king size bed that was obviously too big for the room size. Because of the disproportionate bed size, she had positioned it up against one wall to give the illusion of more space. When we questioned her about the bed, she informed us it was part of the furniture she negotiated in her divorce agreement. The second glaring issue was lack of imagery. Her bedroom was virtually naked when it came to artwork. Finally, she had a very large mirror positioned opposite of her bed.

Recommendations

The first area to hone in on was her bedroom. Whenever you make an adjustment or cure in Feng Shui you should always begin in the bedroom, as this is the room that impacts your life the greatest. Once you successfully adjust this room, work your way outward to the rest of the space focusing on rooms that are utilized most, then address  the property. The resulting changes will impact you personally, then the neighborhood, the community, the state, the country, and finally the universe.

Bedroom

Our first suggestion was to replace the bed and purchase a smaller one. The bed she had was dripping with predecessor energy of a broken relationship and spoiling any potential new relationship. Furthermore, by purchasing a smaller bed she would avoid splitting any future relationship in two, as a king size bed is constructed with two separate parts. The client balked slightly, so we gave her an alternative cure. She could space clear the bed with sage and essential oils and place an intention to remove any problematic energy from it. She then could place a red silk piece of fabric under the mattress along the length of the separation to energetically hold the two pieces together. Finally, we suggested whether she keeps the bed or not, to center it on the wall allowing equal access to her future partner and letting the universe know there is room for two!

The next suggestion was for her to place some artwork within the room. Obviously we wanted her to use imagery and symbolism that suggested romance and pairing qualities, especially in her romance guas, as this would suggest to the universe and anyone entering the space that romance was welcomed in this room.

In terms of the mirror position we recommended it be placed away from reflecting her body while she slept or at least covered at bedtime. Since mirrors are reflective they bounce information and light constantly. The photonic energy created by the mirror interferes with the human aura while asleep resulting in restless sleep patterns. In the end, if we are not well rested it becomes difficult to meet our daily responsibilities, let alone have enough energy to go out and meet new people!

From the bedroom we proceeded to address those rooms she spent most of her time in. We suggested she minimize the amount of horse and female artwork that ensconced her walls and replace it with romantic imagery, particularly in the romance guas. This would suggest to the universe she was ready to open up her life for that special someone.

The garage was the next area to address since it fell into the overall 7-Libra sector of the Euro-Bagua. We needed to stabilize and anchor this space energetically. We accomplished this by forming a grid with Tourmaline stones in the four corners of the space. We also recommended she clear out the clutter and hang a poster or two with a romantic theme. Finally, we moved outward to the property and suggested some landscaping in her 5-Leo, 6-Virgo, and 7-Libra romance guas. Using flowers in varying shades of pink, bench for two, romantic statue, and pairing qualities in plantings, were just some suggestions for her to use in those guas and energetically attract romance into her life.

Results

One week later, the client called and said she had made some initial changes in her bedroom. What she experienced was very exciting for her. She not only seemed to be meeting men easily, but was being asked out on more than one date by the same man!

90

Case Scenario B

*W*e received a call from a young single successful gentleman who proceeded to tell us he was interested in finding "Mrs. Right". He never had trouble meeting women, but as soon as he started dating them for awhile things became really dull, and they all seemed to be bizarre and somewhat secretive. When we evaluated his floor plan there didn't seem to be any glaring issues. Once we arrived for the onsite consultation and began our walk through, we did notice a significant amount of abstract artwork decorating his walls and a great deal of clutter in many of his 8-Scorpio areas. Right away we suggested he minimize and contain the abstract artwork to the 11-Aquarius or 12- Pisces sections of the rooms. Abstract art is very ambiguous and makes for unclear behavior in people. We then suggested he place some fun imagery in the 5-Leo sections throughout the house along with pairing objects in the other relationship guas. We placed a location chart in his bedroom and located his Venus line and suggested he move his bed directly over this planetary line that spews love and beauty. Luckily, the area where the line fell had a workable wall for the bed. Not to fret though, if the bed couldn't be moved over this planetary line because of poor compass direction or layout, then placing an image of love or beauty where the line ran would have been enough to get those energies activated.

*T*o liven up any future relationship we suggested he yang up his space by adding brighter colors or more fire elements, and expose himself to northern and western chi energy. The north relates to winter, a time for lovemaking and the water element that increases deeper emotional feelings for another. The chi energy from the west represents the end of the day and the setting sun which is traditionally related to romance. To achieve this exposure we suggested he place cream colored flowers in the northern sector of his bedroom and red or burgundy colors in the western part of the room. Finally, we recommended he remove all clutter from the 8-Scorpio sections, as the clutter was activating the secretive energies that naturally emanate from this gua, and to go ahead and place some sensual images there instead. Last we heard he was in a serious relationship that we're sure will escalate to marriage!

Case Scenario C

When this client came to us she had been divorced for eight years. She was a single mom raising her daughter who worked as a business consultant. She definitely made an effort to meet men as she worked out at a gym six days a week, attended singles events, and even placed an ad under the dating section of the newspaper. To her dismay, she was unable to meet anyone with marriage potential.

She lived in a townhouse and although the shape of the structure was rectangular, she was missing the right side of her property, as it was attached to another townhouse. Inside was decorated beautifully but we noticed her 5-Leo, 6-Virgo and 7-Libra sections in her main living spaces were inappropriately addressed.

Beginning in her bedroom there were a number of issues. The most glaring was the desk with a computer located in the far right corner or fun relationship gua. Not only was it suggesting her fun was work, but a computer in a bedroom is a major Feng Shui faux pas. Remember, the bedroom is about romance and relaxation, not work! The next issue of concern was the bedroom furniture. You guessed it, from her former marriage just dripping with old memories and being reinforced since she kept her old wedding album stashed under the bed. Her color scheme was appropriate as she did have burgundy and cream colors throughout.

The remaining rooms needed some hint of romance in the associated guas to maximize her romance potential, along with addressing her deck to compensate for the missing right side of her front yard.

Recommendations

Our first suggestion was to remove the wedding album from the premise altogether. She was resistant at first because she felt her daughter should have this memory. We suggested then to give it to her daughter where she could keep it with her possessions. We also suggested she get rid of the bedroom furniture as the predecessor energy of her previous marriage relationship was still present within her life. The next item that needed relocation was the desk and computer. We recommended she move it to the spare bedroom and create an office space for herself. With the empty space in that right hand corner, we suggested an oversized chair for two and this wonderful print she had of a man and woman dancing in the rain.

We also suggested she place two silk roses with the qualities she was looking for in a mate on a scrolled piece of paper and place it in her closet that was located in her 7-Libra commitment section of her room.

In her living room we rearranged her furniture placing the love seat in the far right corner for romance. We also recommended she move her angel drawings from the 7-Libra part of the wall to the 12-Pisces section and place romantic imagery there instead.

Finally, we moved to the outside property to work on compensating for the missing right side of the front yard. We gained it back energetically by addressing the deck as if it represented the entire property. We told her to place two pots together with pink flowers in the right corner of the deck representing partnership and place the intention that her deck now represented her entire yard.

Results

Shortly after her consultation we received a call from this client. She said she sold her bedroom furniture along with some other items she had stored in her garage. She purchased a new bed and some other pieces for the bedroom and moved the desk to the spare room. She adjusted and added a new piece of artwork to the bedroom and living room and had started to work on the deck. The wedding album was tossed as her daughter only wanted one picture from it for her memory box. Shortly after making these adjustments she started meeting men in the strangest places. She found men were reaching out to her at the grocery store, carwash, and her daughter's soccer games. Three months later she called us again and told us she had met a terrific guy at her gym. The funny thing was they must have crossed each others path many times prior, as they both were members at this gym for six years and worked out around the same time in the evening. He asked her for her phone number one night at the gym, one thing led to another, and they are now married!

Case Scenario D

*M*y partner and I had given a seminar on the principles of Feng Shui and it applications in dentistry for an audience of seventy dentists. At the conclusion of the lecture we had several dentists book a consultation not only for their office but their homes as well. One client in particular opened up to us and said she was having a lot of marital problems and if we could come to her home as soon as possible.

*D*uring her phone interview we discovered her husband was a divorce attorney and she spent many hours at her practice. There were three children that in her eyes controlled the household. One of the things noted on her floor plans was a disproportionate ratio of windows to external doors. We also noticed the odd shape architecture that was missing guas 5-Leo, 6-Virgo and most of 7-Libra. We knew right away the chi was stagnant and nonexistent in these crucial relationship areas. When we arrived onsite we were amazed by the amount of artwork with bloody battle scenes of the civil war. Her husband was a history buff and loved civil war memorabilia. The problem was that no matter where you looked there was a bloody battle scene displayed.

*T*he master bedroom was located in the front of the house and filled with clutter from both their jobs. She had a desk filled with patient charts that was located in the marriage Libra section of the room. If that wasn't bad enough, he kept his old client files under their marital bed. Remember, he was a divorce attorney!

*T*he children's bedrooms were located in the back of the house and their doors leading to their rooms were exactly opposite each other or what we call in Feng Shui "biting doors".

Recommendations

The master bedroom is the most important room when it comes to relationships and therefore needs to exude a romantic yin feeling. Because their bedroom was located in the front of the house and contained chaotic items from work, it was overly yang. We suggested they move their bedroom to one of the other rooms located in the rear of the house that was more appropriate for adults.

All work files should be removed and left at their perspective offices or in the home office on the first level. Especially those divorce cases screaming all that negative energy right up through the marital bed. We suggested they incorporate low lighting and romantic color and symbolism within the space.

The next issue to address was the negative imagery of "battle" raging throughout the home. On a subconscious level the family and relationship engaged in these battles on a daily basis. It was time for her husband to keep his collection in his private office space.

The children were controlling the parents primarily because of the window to exterior door ratio. In Feng Shui there should be three windows to every exterior door. The windows not only represent the eyes of the physical body but also represent the voices of the children. The exterior doors on the other hand represent the voice of the parent. The solution here was to make sure all exterior doors functioned properly and looked very auspicious. The final touch was to make sure each exterior door had a chime on it with the largest one place at the front door. Every time the children entered the home it would be a reminder of who was in charge.

The children's bedrooms were also poorly positioned within the home. Since children are yang it is more appropriate for their rooms to be in the front or yang side of the house. A faceted crystal hung in the hallway between the bedroom doors would bring harmony to the biting door arrangement and as a result to the children.

The final area we addressed was the odd shape of the home. We planted two terminating crystals at the point where the length and width of the house would meet if it were squared off. We recommended they either fill in with landscaping or place a lamp post or bird feeder at that same juncture. Internally within those rooms that abut to the missing areas, we suggested they place a mirror or vista along with terminating crystals to energetically push those walls outward. In addition, we recommended they place romantic or pairing imagery in all the 5-Leo, 6-Virgo, and 7-Libra sections of those rooms they occupied with frequency to elevate the chi energy of relationships.

Result

This couple made some changes in their bedroom but simply dropped the ball on the other recommendations. As far as we know they are still together but we are sure much friction still exists. For the relationship to truly flourish they needed to commit to all of the adjustments. We always tell our clients when you are ready you will make the effort to complete the task at hand. Sometimes people are fearful of change and become complacent in their lives no matter how difficult they might be.

Case Scenario E

This particular case study was a client we had
worked with for a prior issue regarding her
career. She contacted us because her personal
life had taken a turn right into the past. She
couldn't figure out why she kept running into old
boyfriends. It got to the point where she had
been set up on a blind date only to arrive and find
an ex-boyfriend staring her in the face. That was
the straw that broke the camels proverbial back and prompted her call to us.

We requested a new set of floor plans from her as she had moved since
her last consultation. There was nothing glaring in terms of the architectural
shape of the home but that was not necessarily the target point we were
looking for. When we dowsed the floor plans it indicated positive for
problematic underground water. We confirmed this finding onsite and
discovered it was passing directly beneath her home. When we questioned
her further about the land, she indicated the development had been built over
swamp land but had been filled by the builders before construction.

Another contributing factor was the boxes of old love letters from previous
boyfriends tucked away in the closet of her spare bedroom that just happened
to be located in the overall 7-Libra section of the house. When we questioned
her further regarding items from
previous relationships, she admitted to
having an assortment of gifts, jewelry
and photos from old lovers.

Recommendations

The first task at hand was to have the client remove all past relationship items from her home. These objects carried the energy from past relationships and as a result pulled her and the ex-boyfriends towards each other. It was important she set an intention during the removal process to close that chapter of her life. A simple ceremonial space clearing with sage and essential oils would complete the process.

Our next concern was the underground water. Not only can underground water be problematic to our health and steal our yang energy, but it pulls us back to the past making it more difficult to let go of items no longer useful to us. It was necessary to dowse out the exact water line direction and place a "mirror sandwich" (one mirror facing downward towards the ground and the other faces upward towards the ceiling), along it to energetically push the water further down into the ground.

Once we addressed the issues that were holding her to the past, we needed to stimulate the chi in the 11-Aquarius section to bring new people into her life. We achieved this by placing a bowl of various colored crystals lying in a bed of sand to generate activity in this gua. Placing a bowl of water in the east direction of her home also activated the energy of new beginnings and vitality needed for a fresh outlook.

We also suggested she add some yang fire elements in the south direction of her home to capitalize on the social energy that naturally emanates from there making it easier for her to be more outgoing.

Result

Remarkably these cures left this client more energized to socialize and meet people; who by the way had no connection to her past!

Case Scenario F

We wanted to share this next client example with our readers even though it does not deal with a relationship on a personal basis. It is important to remember we can treat the 7-Libra section from a business perspective as well. We will not delve too deeply here with business Feng Shui as we will leave that for another book.

This client owned a financial consulting firm with four other partners. One of their main complaints was the constant friction between them. It seemed that every decision that needed to be made, even on the smallest level, ended in a four way dispute. The floor plan design was very disjointed causing the partners' offices to be separated across the building. When we arrived for the onsite consultation we were taken aback by all the sports memorabilia on the walls. The art was an expensive collection depicting many different sporting events; however, the main theme was boxing. By the looks of the office my partner and I could have sworn we were in a sports agency rather than a financial firm. As we continued to walk the space we noted the partners offices also contained this type of imagery, but even worst yet, many of the boxing pictures were placed on their partnership wall. In other words, they were literally knocking themselves out!

Recommendations

The first suggestion to this client was to remove the majority of sports memorabilia. In Feng Shui it is very important the imagery pertain to how the space is being utilized. In this case the client owned a financial firm, not a sporting company.

The lobby was the first area they needed to place financial imagery and remove the sporting artwork. In addition to the lobby area being addressed, we recommended all partner offices have imagery pertaining to the company services, along with symbolism depicting partnering energy or duality, and placed on their partnership wall (middle third of the right wall upon entry).

By changing visually what the partners saw each day would gain focus on their company and draw them in the same direction. The final recommendation in assisting the partners in seeing eye-to-eye was to form a grid with their offices. We accomplished this by positioning two of the partner offices in the overall 3-Gemini section of the building and placing the remaining two partners in the overall 7-Libra section of the building. By doing this we locked the energy of **"communication"** with the **"partnership"**.

One last recommendation we had was to make sure their new artwork had metal frames with glass fronts, and a metal chime or mirror placed in all the 3-Gemini sections of their offices. The reflectivity from these objects would aid in effective communication between them. Last we heard this company not only improved their sales by 150%, but the partners actually could get through a meeting without an argument!

Case Scenario G

This is a scenario we hear often when dealing with our Feng Shui relationship clients. The old "he doesn't want to commit syndrome". We previously worked with this particular client on her romance issue. She obviously had done a good job as she was ecstatic about the man she was with. The only problem is they had been seeing each other for over two years and no indication of a committed future on his part. Now two years is not an eternity but when the couple in question are in their mid forties, that's a different story.

Since this client was totally committed to the relationship and wanted to marry this man, our Feng Shui focus was on him. We recommended she increase his exposure to some northwestern chi energy, since that direction is associated with fatherly wisdom and planning ahead. In order for this client to expose her lover to more of this directional energy, we suggested she place metal elements in that direction of her home and especially in those rooms he spent a great deal of time in. In addition, we recommended she place a picture of the two of them in an oval metal frame and place it on his desk at the office along with a metal vase with white roses in this same direction. It was also important this client yang up their space by keeping it organized, well lit, brighter colors, and placing wind chimes in any stagnant corners. As a result the chi becomes playful and alert , impacting their personal chi giving them a more decisive outspoken behavior.

We also suggested he wear more metal colors like off white, grey, silver or gold so he personally would absorb the energy of the metal directions to help him relax yet be responsible and decisive.

Result

This client was so excited to place her cures that she addressed the northwestern quadrant of not only the entire house but in every room as well. She also bought him some ties with metal colors and more white shirts so when he was away from home he could still absorb the energy of the northwest. She even went so far as to include more yang foods within his diet like fish, root vegetables, and chicken to help him be more assertive and decisive. According to her, when she brings up the issue of marriage he takes part in the conversation enthusiastically!

Case Scenario H

This case scenario deals with several issues within a marriage. The main issue was the constant bickering between her and her husband. Because of this arguing at times she felt rather intimidated by her husband leaving her tense and short-tempered. In her opinion, much of the problem stemmed from them barely seeing each other because of the hectic pace they kept. With these type of issues we decided to hone in on directional and planetary energy with proper imagery.

The first issue we addressed was the incessant arguing. We noticed the atmosphere of their home was chaotic and not very relaxing that subconsciously was making them feel on edge. We recommended they remove the clutter and tone down the overly yang colors to create a more yin or relaxing environment. Greens, blues, creams and other pastel color accents would do the trick. Wooden or bamboo furniture would also help to slow down chi and create a softer, more relaxing space, along with softening any sharp angles with plants or pillows.

When we questioned the client if there was a particular room where they argued most, they both responded, "the bedroom!" When we took compass direction it revealed their heads were pointing south when they slept. Southern energy with sleep is highly problematic. First, it was contributing to their argumentative behavior because the directional energy is very yang and lends itself to tension. Secondly, when we sleep with our heads pointing south, over time it will flip our own electromagnetic field that naturally travels up our back, over the top of our heads, and down the front of our body. The reason this happens is we are in direct opposition to the earth's electromagnetic field that comes out of the north pole and back through to the south pole. When our fields are flipped everything is more difficult for us including staying healthy. Finally, when we placed their location chart in the center of the room we found a Mars planetary line running right down the middle of the bed. Mars is a planetary energy that is aggressive and energetic; definitely a line that will incite arguments. The easiest solution here was to move the bed! We suggested they position the bed on the north wall so as to align their own energy field with that of the earth's. This also moved them off the problematic Mars line. In addition to Mars being a problematic line to sleep on, Uranus, Jupiter, Pluto and Saturn will also present difficulties. Uranus is about sudden changes and eccentricity, so when we are trying to sleep over this type of energy we tend to wake up suddenly throughout the night and as a result will suffer from sleep deprivation. Pluto has a very isolating and transformational energy attached to it. As a result one feels very lonely when sleeping on this line even if they are sharing their bed with another. Jupiter is the planet of expansion so any problem you take to bed will grow with intensity and have you tossing all night long. Saturn is the planet of responsibility and inflexibility. Sleeping on this type of energy will make you stiff physically as well as emotionally. Obviously, not a very good line for romance.

As part of our Feng Shui services, we are able to determine if a client is being affected by a problematic planetary energy by placing a location chart in the center of the home or room. The chart is constructed from the client's birth data and determines where the planets were overhead exactly the moment of birth. This planetary energy becomes imprinted on the auric field of the individual and thus the location chart can be brought to any location where the individual lives.

We now wanted the wife to align herself with more yang energy to help her overcome her feelings of intimidation by her spouse. We recommended she dress in brighter yang colors to activate the yang qualities along with eating a diet rich in yang foods. Plenty of fish, chicken, thick soups, and root vegetables. We also wanted to calm her husband's overwhelming personality by subduing the chi energy within him. Encouraging him to eat more yin foods such as salads, fruits and juices along with relaxing exercises like yoga and Tai Chi.

Finally, we needed to encourage a relaxing western and southwestern chi to facilitate a home oriented feeling and focus their energies on the relationship. By incorporating more earth elements such as crystals, stones, or clay pots in the southwest direction of their family room would encourage a feeling of warm contentment.

Result

Almost immediately after moving their bed and adjusting their diets the arguing significantly decreased. Once this component was no longer a factor in the marriage, she said the other adjustments flowed with ease. They are both enjoying their new found time together and love the feel to their home!

Obviously we could go on and on with different case scenarios, but we think you have the gist of how Feng Shui can impact ones' life and the issues that an individual may be experiencing at one particular time or another. The harmony and balance that this wonderful art and science brings to our own lives as well as our clients is not only fascinating but truly rewarding.

9
How Compatible Are You With Your Partner ?

How Compatible Are You With Your Partner?

*W*ouldn't it be nice to see how compatible you are with your partner by simple plugging in a few numbers into a formula? Well, conceptually it is that easy but theoretically this system of compass school Feng Shui is quite involved. The Compass school approach to Feng Shui is very powerful and works on a highly sophisticated level. In particular, the Eight House System believes the eight cardinal directions hold a unique chi energy that is either positive or negative to an individual. Obviously, you want to capitalize on the chi directional energies that are beneficial to you and minimize the time spent in those directions that are considered problematic for you. In addition to this system determining how compatible you are with another person, it can also determine how compatible you are with your home.

*E*ssentially the theory breaks down to a formula known as the East/ West Group. This formula divides the 8 trigrams of the bagua into two groups. The Trigrams represent 8 basic universal images: Thunder, Wind, Fire, Earth, Marsh or Lake, Heaven or Sky, Water, and Mountain. Before any language was written, symbols were used to describe these images. These symbols were trigrams. The solid line represented motion, elevation, hard and bold images, whereas the broken lines represented motionless, soft, depressed and weak images. Later, people called the solid line *Yang* and the broken line *Yin*.

East Group:		West Group	
Trigram	Direction	Trigram	Direction
Zhen: Thunder	East	Qian: Heaven	Northwest
Xun: Wind	Southeast	Dui: Lake	West
Li: Fire	South	Gen: Mountain	Northeast
Kan: Water	North	Kun: Earth	Southwest

Bagua

When using the East/West Compass Formula we can determine which group we belong to. Once we determined whether we are an east group or west group person, we then know what directions are favorable for us. Basically, if you belong to an east group all four of the associated directions are favorable for you, whereas the directions of the west group are unfavorable. If you belong to the west group then the associated directions for that group are favorable for you while the east group directions are unfavorable. It then becomes evident that if you fall into an east group you are more compatible with a person who also belongs to this same group.

In order to determine if you belong to either the east group or west group you need to figure out your personal Trigram or Ming Kua number. There are a couple of rules to keep in mind however before computing your Ming Kua. If your birthday falls in the month of January through February 3rd or 4th, you must subtract 1 from your birth year. The calculations are based on the Chinese solar calendar that uses the beginning of spring , (February 4th or 5th) to mark the beginning of the year. This is based on the solstice and vernal equinox. So for example, if a female was born January 8, 1989, the year 1988 would be used in calculating the Ming Kua.

Calculation Steps:

1. Check to see if the birth date was prior to the Chinese new year on February 4th or 5th. If so, subtract 1 from the year since the Chinese calendar recognizes the birth year to be the previous year.

2. Take your birth year and add together all the digits: 1961 $1+9+6+1 = 17$.

3. If the result is greater than 9, add the digits together again. 17 is greater than 9, so add its digits together; $1+7= 8$.

4. If you are male, subtract the result from 11; if you are female add the result to 4. So for males subtract the result from 11: 8-11= 3. For females add the result to 4: 8+4=12.

5. If the result is greater than 9, add its digits together again. Male = 3 No need. Female = 12 Needs calculation, so 1+2=3.

6. If the answer is 5, the kua number is 2 for a male, or 8 for a female. If this does not apply then the kua number is the answer from the previous step, so in this case 3.

Once you have determined your personal Ming Kua number you can locate your personal trigram. If we were to continue with our example of **3** being the personal kua number for an individual born in 1961, the personal trigram of Zhen relating to thunder and the east direction on the bagua becomes your personal trigram. Of course there are many other characteristics of Zhen such as family member, body parts and other qualities but for the purpose of this book we will focus on the directional energy.

If you refer to the East Group chart you will see that trigram Zhen falls under this group and there are 4 good directions associated with it. These directions are east, southeast, south and north. There are also four unfavorable directions for the east group person and they are simply the four favorable directions for the west group individual. Therefore, southwest, west, northwest and northeast are the problematic directions for an east group individual. On the flip side, the four favorable directions for a west group individual are southwest, west, northwest and northeast and the problematic directions for this group are east, southeast, south and north. To make a long story short, kua numbers 1,3,4 and 9 fall into the east group and kua numbers 2,6,7 and 8 fall into a west group.

The quick reference chart below will assist you in locating your good and bad directions. Take special note of the direction to face for relationships. By placing your bedroom or bed in this direction can bring harmony to the partnership. However, there is one direction we do not want your head to face when you sleep. The south direction is in direct opposition to the earth's electromagnetic field flow and because of this, over time there is the possibility of your own magnetic field to flip resulting in a plethora of health issues. If your best direction for relationships is south, you can choose a south bedroom or just spend time together in this direction rather than placing your bed in this direction.

	East Group				West Group			
Kua #	3	4	1	9	6	2	8	7
1	S	N	SE	E	W	NE	SW	NW
2	SE	E	S	N	SW	NW	W	NE
3	N	S	E	SE	NE	W	NW	SW
4	E	SE	N	S	NW	SW	NE	W
P-1	SW	NW	W	NE	SE	E	S	N
P-2	NE	W	NW	SW	N	S	E	SE
P-3	NW	SW	NE	W	E	SE	N	S
P-4	W	NE	SW	NW	S	N	SE	E

1 - Prosperity	P-1 Arguments
2 - Romantic Relationships	P-2 Failed Relationships
3 - Good Health	P-3 Accidents
4 - Peace & Stability	P-4 Misfortune

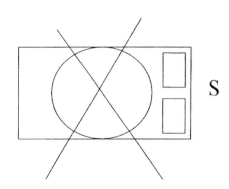

S

* P stands for problematic

As you can see the favorable directions for each group are directly opposite. Because of this you may find it easier to live with someone who shares your group orientation. The major conflict arises with sleeping positions and the Chai Kua or house group. In this scenario we will generally align the "bread winner" to the favorable direction and house group and place remedies for other occupants with differing directions.

The Chai Kua or house group is a way to determine the compatibility with your home. Essentially, the group a house falls into is based on its sitting compass direction (opposite of how it faces). In order to determine the sitting compass direction, simply take a compass reading from your front door or facing direction and look directly opposite of that direction to determine your sitting direction. For example, if you stand at your front door or facing direction with your back towards this direction while you look out towards the street and note the compass direction reading, let's say 90 degrees east, then your sitting direction is exactly 180 degrees opposite, or 270 degrees west. A few important things to note when taking a compass reading. First, make sure you are not wearing metal on your person or standing near metal, this includes cars and telephone poles. Secondly, hold the compass at waist level in a relaxed, flexed-knee position. Finally, determine your facing direction of your house by noting the open area in front. Some homes have a front door to the side that actually faces a neighbors wall of their house or some kind of an obstruction. In this case your facing direction may be the window that faces the street or open yard.

Facing Position ←  **Sitting Position**

Once you have determined your Chai Kua or house group, compare it to your personal kua number. Obviously, an east group individual would feel best in an east group house! Using these formulas gives you and your partner just one more advantage for a harmonious, successful relationship.

Enjoy the easy reference chart below to determine the group orientation of your home. Remember, the group is determined by the sitting position of the home.

Sitting Position	Facing Position	House Trigram	Element	East/West Group
S	N	Li	Fire	East
SW	NE	Kun	Earth	West
W	E	Dui	Metal	West
NW	SE	Qian	Metal	West
N	S	Kan	Water	East
NE	SW	Gen	Earth	West
E	W	Zhen	Wood	East
SE	NW	Xun	Wood	East

House Groups & Trigrams

* Remember to compare the house group with your personal kua number group.

Glossary of Terms

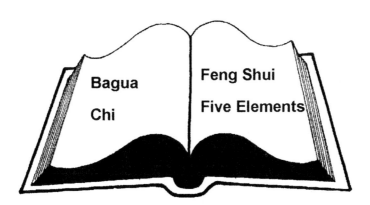

Bagua

Feng Shui

Chi

Five Elements

Glossary of Feng Shui Terms

Aries - One of the 12 astrological signs of the zodiac. Aries qualities include aggressive behavior, a childlike curiosity and playfulness, resilient innocence, and a restless wild spirit.

Aquarius - Aquarius rules the circulatory system, calves and ankles. Aquarian qualities include an ability to see the big picture, a casual friendly nature, mental acuity (even brilliance), and inventiveness.

Astro* Carto*Graphy - Where Feng Shui concerns itself with creating harmony in the immediate home environment by removing obstacles, moving furniture and use of color and symbols. Astro*Carto*Graphy deals with the most harmonious places in the world to live.

Bagua - Also translated as Pa kua, the eight-sided symbol that is said to have been inspired centuries ago by the markings on a tortoise shell, that defines the directions and the various energies associated with them. The bagua is an indispensable tool in Feng Shui depicting the human life experience.

Baubiologie - Also known as Bio-Architecture, it is the study of the influence of the habitat on living creatures. It includes the geography both on and under the surface of the earth, the weather, and the materials used to construct and decorate a building, the electromagnetic fields, and various other factors. Dowsing is one method used to determine which of these elements influence your well-being and your health.

Black Hat Sect - Black Hat Sect Feng Shui is a school of thought that is most widely practiced in the USA founded by spiritual leader Grand Master Thomas Lin Yun. It combines the principles of Feng Shui design with spiritually, psychology of modern science and the transcendental to reflect the needs of the society today.

Cancer- Cancerian qualities include powerful, tempestuous emotions, or moods, a fierce protectiveness of family, a strong ability to nurture others, and a resistance to external change. The body part representation is the breast and belly.

Capricorn - Capricorn rules the knees, bones, and skin. The qualities of Capricorn include an ability to earn and manage money, a strong sense of responsibility, reliability, steady, unflappable emotions, and cautious sensibilities.

Chi - Dragon's Breath, the life-giving forces of the universe. This is the general term for energy, which is everywhere, in everything. Feng Shui concerns itself with the movement and manipulation of chi with the goal being to create a more positive life experience.

Contemporary Western Feng Shui - Basically places the Bagua according to the location of the front door and it has a very solid foundation in ancient "form" school principles. Contemporary western Feng Shui focuses on creating a nourishing flow of "chi" (life force energy) through the home, and correcting intangible factors such as "predecessor chi". It puts strong emphasis on the client's intentions for change and growth, recognizing that we are powerfully connected to our environment on a quantum level.

Compass School - Compass School principles are based on the I Ching. It divides the home into 8 trigrams known as the Pakua and analyses the energy flow in the home. The eight trigrams are, family, abundance, fame/future, marriage, children/creativity, helpful people & travel, career and knowledge/wisdom.

Crystals - Considered very auspicious in Feng Shui because of their ability to attract and amplify positive energy or chi through diffusion of light.

Diving Rod - A forked rod (or sometimes a pair of L-shaped rods) used in dowsing.

Earth - This element is at the center of the eight trigrams and is in the opposing directions of southwest and northeast. Its colors are earth tones, yellows, or tans. This elemental qi is responsible for wealth and money.

Earth Energy Grids - The Earth's energy grid can be thought of as a web that holds or links the Earth together. The energy grid is affected by many influences - electricity, magnetism, light, color, heat, sound and matter. The planetary energy grid operates through certain geometrical patterns that follow a specific symmetry. The grids meet at various intersecting points forming a kind of matrix. This is equivalent to the acupressure points on our bodies. These grid points can be found at some of the strongest power places on the planet.

East - One of the compass points on the bagua grid. It is associated with the color green, element of wood, family life area, and its main character is contentment.

Eight Trigrams - The set of trigrams used to make up the bagua. A symbolic representation of the family, time, and seasons.

Eight Houses Theory - A school of Feng Shui that uses a static view of a home, office, or area, and examines the effects intangible forces have on the occupants.

Electromagnetic Frequency - Any frequency within the electromagnetic spectrum associated with radio wave propagation. When a radio frequency current is supplied to an antenna, an electromagnetic field is created that then is able to propagate through space. Many wireless technologies are based on RF (radio frequency) field propagation. These frequencies make up part of the electromagnetic radiation spectrum.

Elements - The essence of Feng Shui is rooted in the interaction and balance between the five elements, which are water, wood, fire, metal, and earth. Each of these elements governs particular aspects of life.

Energy - The practice of Feng Shui concerns itself with the movement and quality of energy, or chi, in a space. Creating a healthy and positive flow of energy is said to enhance physical and emotional health and quality of life.

Euro-Bagua - Highly sophisticated map for analyzing a current life situation through the environment by combining the traditional 8 parted bagua map with western mystery traditions.

Feng - Literally means "wind".

Feng Shui - Literally translated as wind/water and said to be over 5000 years old, the art of Feng Shui concerns itself with the movement and quality of energy, or chi, which is present everywhere, in everything. By consciously manipulating this energy through various techniques and symbolism that have evolved over time, it is thought that all areas of one's life experience can be affected in a profoundly positive way.

Fight or Fight - A primitive involuntary reaction triggered during moments of danger or anxiety.

Fire - One of the five elements, the fire sector is located in the south. It is energized by the colors red, purple, magenta, pink and orange. Objects such as candles, incense burners, lamps and fireplaces are perfect in this area.

Five Elements - Wood, Fire, Earth, Metal, and Water. These elements are the foundation theory for Feng Shui balance. These variables have a productive, reductive and destructive cycle.

Five Phases - Five physical elements in nature that represent the movement of chi. They are fire, earth, metal, water and wood. The concept of the five phases is the backbone of Chinese medicine, acupuncture and Feng Shui.

Flying Stars - Can be described as astrology of the home. A chart of "stars" or numbers is defined based on year of construction and facing direction. Some number combinations are good, some unlucky. Feng Shui "cures" use the five elements to counteract, defuse, or correct unlucky star combinations. These star combinations change annually and monthly influences can be looked at as well.

Four Pillars of Destiny - According to ancient Chinese philosophy, a person's life is altered by the date and time of birth (Ba-Zi). Ancient Chinese devised a method of reading the life of a person from his birth year, month, day, and hour. This information is displayed in the form of four columns each consisting of two characters. Each column is called a Pillar. The four pillars together will contain eight characters. This method of Life Reading is called The Four Pillars of Destiny or simply The Eight Characters.

Form School - Oldest practice of Feng Shui and influenced by natural geography and is the oldest practice of Feng Shui. The phoenix, dragon, tortoise and tiger are symbolic animals, which aid in the Feng Shui principles of placement.

Geomancy - (From the Latin *geo*, "Earth," *mancy* "prophecy") has always been a method of divination that interprets markings on the ground or how handfuls of dirt land when you toss them.

Geopathic Stress - Geopathic stress is "an abnormal energy field generated underground by mineral deposits, water streams, or geological faults."

Gemini - Gemini rules the hands. Its qualities include a quick mind, communication, expression and an ability to see many facets of a given issue.

I Ching - Great Philosophical Book of Changes governing all movements and developments of every event or phenomenon in the universe. An ancient Chinese system of divination.

Integrative Feng Shui - The beauty of Feng Shui is that as the earth and her people change, grow and develop so does the Feng Shui. Integrative Feng Shui is simply a combination of all the different discipline schools of Feng Shui. The incorporation of form school, compass school, astrology, numerology, geomancy and western Feng Shui are some of the disciplines practiced when integrating Feng Shui.

Intuitive Feng Shui - Everyone has the ability intuitively to pinpoint exactly what is out of balance within his or her environment and then make a change for the better. By meditating and listening to your inner voice we can all understand our environment on an intuitive level and as a result make cures to naturally enhance our spaces.

Jupiter - Relates to higher education, expansion, growth, philosophy, luck, success and achievement. It rules the abstract mind and the astrological signs of Sagittarius and Pisces.

Leo - Leo rules the heart and spine. Leo qualities include affectionate warmth, an outgoing nature, an imperial bearing, aggressive self-expression, and generosity of spirit.

Ley Lines - Alignments and patterns of powerful, invisible earth energy said to connect various sacred sites, such as churches, temples, stone circles, megaliths, holy wells, burial sites, and other locations of spiritual importance.

Libra - Libra rules the lower back and hips. The Libran qualities include physical beauty, strong sensuality, artistic sensibilities, tact and diplomacy, and an innate sense of fairness and balance.

Location Chart – An astrological technique showing exactly where each planet was passing overhead at the time of birth printed out on a compass wheel diagram.

Lo Shu Grid - A 3 by 3 pattern, as found on the back of a giant tortoise shell.

Lou Pan / Lo Pan - A Chinese compass used to determine the flow of chi for determining the orientation of buildings, rooms, and furniture.

Luo Shu - The magic square containing the 9 stars.

Luck - Is comprised of three components known as Heaven Luck, Earth Luck and Man Luck.

Mars - Represents dynamic expression, aggression, individualism and competitiveness. This energy can be constructive or destructive depending on how it is channeled. Mars rules Aries and Scorpio.

Mercury - It is the messenger and speaks in terms of logic and reasoning. It represents how we think and communicate. It rules the astrological sign Gemini.

Metal - One of the five elements, the sector governed by metal is in the north/ northwest sector of the space. Metal energy is activated by the colors silver, gold and white.

Ming Gua - Life gua station or experience.

Moon - Your inner self or intuition. It is the feminine, the mother, ultimate yin. Symbolically the moon represents our ability to become part of the whole. It rules the astrological sign of cancer.

Neptune - Is about your illusions, spiritual insight, psychic ability, the unconscious mind, dreams and mystical experiences. It goes beyond the ego. It rules the astrologic sign Pisces.

North - This direction is energized by the water element, and can be energized by the use of colors such as blue, green and aqua. Water features such as fountains and aquariums will be very effective in this area.

Northeast - One of the compass points on the bagua grid. It is associated with the color blue, element of earth, knowledge life area, and its main character is motivation.

Numerology - The study of numbers, and the occult manner in which they reflect certain aptitudes and character tendencies, as an integral part of the cosmic plan.

Pakua - An octagon shaped amulet, consisting of eight sections, sometimes called the Eight Trigrams.

Pendulum - An apparatus consisting of an object mounted so that it swings 360 degrees freely under the influence of gravity.

Personal Trigram – Determined by your birth year and gender.

Phoenix - The symbolic animal of Form School that lies in the south compass point. It is represented by the summer and the color red.

Pisces - Pisceans are gentle, patient, compassionate, charitable and quickly put the needs of others ahead of their own. Pisces rules the feet, liver and lymphatic system.

Poison Arrow - Poison arrow is a term that refers to sharp, hostile corners or objects, both indoors and out, that cause an abundance of oppressive energy, or sha chi, to be directed at the inhabitants of a space.

Qi - (Mandarin) - Also known as chi; vital energy; primordial breath; air; breath, energy. Qi, in reference to the human body, is considered yang. According to the Scholar Warrior Dictionary, [qi is] a Yang counterpart to Blood (Yin), it forms and circulates blood (refer to San Bao).

Sagittarius - Sagittarius rules the hips and thighs. Sagittarian qualities include an unshakeable devotion to the concept and practice of truth, a hearty sense of adventure, a love of variety and difference, an affable extroverted nature, and a drive to explore.

Saturn - This planet provides structure, discipline, responsibility and restrictions. It holds the key in what is to be accomplished in life. It rules Capricorn and Aquarius.

Scorpio - Scorpio rules the genitals. The qualities of Scorpio include: a lifelong fascination with sex, birth, and death, an extremely focused nature, penetrative insight, a strong sense of privacy, and an ability to subtly affect others in profound (often sexual) way.

Sheng - Life, growth, beneficial.

Sha Chi - Also known as killing breath, sha chi refers to the negative energy that is caused by sharp angles and hostile structures.

Sheng Chi - An upward moving flow of positive chi. This is the chi we strive to have in our homes and our bodies.

Shui - Literally means "water."

South - This direction is governed by fire and rules the areas of fame and reputation. Placing red objects, and burning candles and incense in this area will improve public opinion and bring opportunities to be in the public's eye.

Southeast - This direction is governed by the wood element and rules the area of wealth. Energize and activate your financial life by placing plants or a water element in this area, and by using the colors of the earth such as green, brown and ochre.

Southwest - This direction is governed by earth and rules the area of romance. It will be beneficial to use the color red in this sector, as well as pink, purple and orange as fire creates earth. Pyramid and triangular shaped objects and lit candles and incense are also energizing to this area along with earth elements such as crystals, stones, marble, terracotta, etc.

Space Clearing - Space (or energy/vibrations) does not stop at walls or furniture. The vibrations also run through seemingly solid objects and gives them a history. This history has energy patterns that can be perceived. The history could be one of joy and laughter, or it could be of sadness and loneliness and even of tragedy. The history can be made up of past events from our own lives in a place, or they can be made from the experiences of previous occupants and people who have worked on the dwelling. What we do in space clearing is manipulate the space so that any negative or unwanted energetic elements of the history of the structure are removed. For example: divorce, death, illness, bankruptcy, etc.

Sun - Also known as Surya and Aditya, Sun is the ruler of all the planets. The sun is believed to be the source of vitality and the physical make up. It is responsible for the success, intellect, wisdom, fortune, fame and wealth. The sun is the ruler of the zodiac sign Leo.

Taoism - A philosophy and religion based on the I Ching.

Taurus: Taurus is associated with the classical earth element, and thus called an Earth Sign (with Virgo and Capricorn). Taurus rules the neck and shoulders. Taurean qualities include an earthy, practical nature, a love of luxury and a devotee of sensuality, strong opinions, and a profound stubbornness.

Tiger - A symbolic animal of the Form School that sits in the west. It represents autumn and the color white.

Tortoise - A symbolic animal of the Form School. It represents winter, the color black, and compass point north.

Uranus - Represents innovation, breaks in tradition, sudden changes, genius, inventions and eccentricity. It rules the zodiac sign Aquarius.

Venus - It governs beauty, love, artistic instinct and the ability to attract compatible people to us. It rules the astrological signs of Taurus and Libra.

Virgo - Virgo rules the intestines. Virgo qualities include an ability to organize, attention to cleanliness, extreme restlessness, selflessness, a desire for service, and an ability to get things done.

Water - Symbolic of wealth and prosperity, water features placed in the north within the home are the most auspicious, with the southeast and southwest being secondary locations. Fountains are very good water features because the moving water has fewer tendencies to become stagnant than sitting bowls of water, which may also be used as long as they are kept very fresh.

West - This direction is governed by the metal element and rules the area of children and creativity. White, silver and gold are good colors to use here, and metal objects like bells, bowls and sculptures are energizing to this sector.

Wind Chimes - Considered to create very positive chi, wind chimes are appropriate in a number of circumstances. The material that chime is made of will determine where it should best be placed. Metal chimes should be placed in the west/northwest; bamboo or wood chimes in the east/southeast and ceramic in the southwest/northeast. In all cases, wind chimes are useful for dispersing sha chi and for generating and heightening the movement of positive chi.

Wood - One of the five elements, wood is represented by the east, which rules family and health and by the southeast, which rules wealth in the classical 8 parted system. Wood objects and live plants are auspicious in these areas, as are the colors brown, beige and green. Red should be avoided in these areas, since fire, (red) drains the wood.

Yang -Yang energy is the active half of the yin-yang concept. It is symbolized by light, activity, movement rigidity and strength. It is also associated with male energy. It must always be balanced with similarly opposite levels of yin energy.

Yin - Yin energy is the passive half of the yin-yang concept. It is symbolized by darkness, stillness, flexibility and weakness and is associated with female energy. It must be balanced in all situations by an equal presence of yang energy.

Zen - To figure out something by meditation or by a sudden flash of enlightenment.

Appendix A

Astro* Carto* Graphy® & Location Charts

Now that you have completed this book and made all your Feng Shui adjustments and found that perfect partner, it's time to find the best place to live! Astro* Carto* Graphy® is an astrological technique for locating the most harmonious place on earth for you to buy your lovely abode. How can that be? Well, planetary energy has a tremendous impact on our behavior and as a result plays a significant role in how balanced we feel. Astro* Carto* Graphy® is an actual map of the world showing exactly where the planets and major asteroids were positioned the moment you were born. Therefore, whatever area in the world a pleasant planetary line is positioned for you personally, your energy will be naturally draw to it. In other words, have you ever felt you could live in a particular state or country that you had visited on vacation? Most likely this place had your Sun or Moon line running right through it and left you with a very nurturing or comfortable feeling.

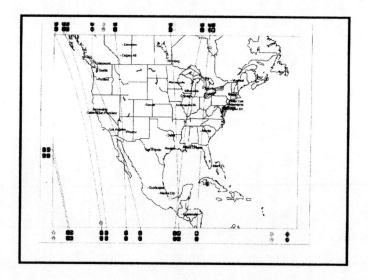

Some of the most favorable planetary lines are the Sun, Jupiter, Venus, Mercury and the Moon. These planets generally are quite complementary for us in life. In short, the Sun line makes you feel most centered and protected while being rather creative. It is your central point of the self.

Jupiter is very expansive in its size and energy and tends to have that effect on our personality. We feel very optimistic and bold on our Jupiter line which is quite helpful when planning our future.

Venus ensconces us with beauty, love and sensitivity. These are certainly very attractive qualities for one to gravitate towards.

Mercury has a very playful, intellectual and communicative energy. We interact with others very well on this line as it is very flexible or mutable in nature. And finally, a moon line provides us with that motherly nurturing quality we all need in life. It is a soothing line that carries an abundance of emotional energy with it.

Now of course we need to take the good with the bad, so to speak. Saturn, Mars, Pluto, Uranus and Neptune can be rather problematic planetary energies. Saturn is considered to be the planet of structure and responsibility. Obviously there are instances in life where we need to have this type of disciplined energy, but to have it continually can become burdensome and depressing.

Mars carries an aggressive, independent and head-strong energy with it. The tendency is to be overly competitive and aggressive on this line causing arguments and hostility.

*P*luto is the furthest planet from the sun and therefore very isolating and cold, to say the least. It is considered the planet of transformational energies and that is just what your life is filled with when living on this planetary line. It also can wreak havoc on the immune system and predispose one to more serious conditions like cancers.

*U*ranus is very innovative, inventive in nature, and rather eccentric. Although these qualities seem exciting, they can be too erratic making life a bit bizarre.

*N*eptune can be creative and spiritual but also rather illusionary. It can be a line that lures you into being unrealistic that over time can be rather problematic.

*N*ow, once you know these planetary energies you can analyze a Astro* Carto* Graphy® Map or Location Chart and determine the best state or country to reside in along with the best room to place your desk or bed in. Remember, sometimes we are drawn to more problematic planetary lines during certain periods in our life in order to accomplish a particular goal or challenge.

Location Charts

A location chart works on a smaller level and can be applied to any space you move into. Like the Astro* Carto* Graphy®, the location chart shows where the planets and major asteroids were positioned at the moment of birth. This information is then displayed on a printed compass wheel and aligned to true north within a home, building or room indicating where the planets fall into that space. For example, you may want to place your telephone or computer on a Mercury line or position your bed on a Venus line.

*T*he benefits of these astrological techniques are countless. Once you fully understand the energies that the planets possess, you can then determine the most favorable place to live or rooms to occupy.

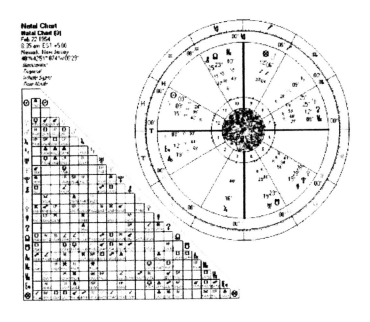

Appendix B

Mary Jane and Shelley are the owners of Harmonious Living Feng Shui consulting firm. They practice a unique integrative form of Feng Shui where one is able to explore their true destination in life. Their firm offers an array of services and products for the public, student and practitioner. Listed below are some services and products offered by their company. For more information about various products, lectures and workshop topics visit their website: www.harmoniousliving4u.com.

Services

Singles or Spoken For: We tour your home and give you specific recommendations & affirmations on how you can attract love into your life or enhance it. Our main focus is to activate the love aspects of your home-especially the love sectors of the bedroom.

Weddings: Beginning your lifetime together with balance and a positive flow of energy is a powerful way to create the foundation for a strong, healthy and happy marriage. Harmonious Living can draft a Bagua Map of your location so that you can plan for the best placement of décor, activity areas and seating arrangements including how to: Energize your Love & Marriage zone and stimulate your Wealth zone.

Feng Shui Party: Form a group of 10 or more people for a 1½ hour presentation. You and your friends will learn the basics of Feng Shui-what it means, and how to apply the Bagua Map to your home or office. Harmonious Living provides attendees with practical Feng Shui tips you can use right away.

Feng Shui Real Estate: Are you buying the right property? Are you having difficulty selling your property? Are you planning on building a new home or office? These are just some of the important questions to ask yourself about real estate. Harmonious Living Feng Shui is the perfect medicine for what ails the potential buyer or seller as our approach is all about making a house feel good for that potential buyer.

Feng Shui For Children: Children and parents can enjoy success and healthy relationships if the environment energetically supports them. Applying Feng Shui is a practical tool for parents and anyone concerned with children, not only for creating spaces where children can thrive, but to understand them better.

Space Clearing: For your life to work well, it is vital to have a good flow of clear, vibrant energy in your home and workplace. Harmonious Living uses a variety of space clearing techniques that work on a deep level to transform stagnant predecessor energy and restore balance to the occupants lives.

Onsite & Phone Consultations: Whether it is for your personal residence or business, we offer a comprehensive service including written reports, location charts, flying star analysis, numerology and other solutions to bring about the results you are looking for.

Dowsing & Earth Acupuncture: Areas of powerful earth energy (ley lines or underground water) are problematic to our health. Dowsing these points and adjusting the vibrational flow through earth acupuncture makes it healthier for us to live near these energies.

Educational Programs: We offer various workshops on Feng Shui topics for local community programs, colleges, and professional organizations. For a detailed list of courses visit our website: www.harmoniousliving4u.com.

Feng Shui Certificate Program: This is a 12-month comprehensive certification course blending Eastern and Western Feng Shui principles including compass and form school theories, numerology, astrology and earth energies.

Products

Educational Tapes: For those of you who wish to gain a greater understanding of Feng Shui and learn how to implement this science in your homes and business these audio tapes are a great way to learn. Every time you re-listen to the tapes there is always something new to pick up. Each class contains 120 minutes of audio information combined with worksheets. For a list of audio tape topics visit our website: www.harmoniousliving4u.com.

Pure Essential Oils: Feng Shui is all about moving beneficial energy to where it will do you the most good. Pure essential oils is a great way to energetically boost the chi in those areas you specifically want to enhance. We work with Nature's Sunshine oils because of their high quality and purity. Ordering oils from NSP call 1-800-453-1422 and reference # 1470317-3.

Electromagnetic Pollution: Our bodies can become easily disrupted from the problematic electromagnetic frequency fields emitted from appliances and man-made structures within the environment. We carry products such as Crystal Catalyst Beads, Electronic Smog Buster Tabs, Cellular Phone Tabs, Tri-Paks, Resonators, and Pendants, which are made from a unique composition (space age ceramics) and structure allowing them to absorb and then rebroadcast harmful electromagnetic radiations in a cleaner form for the human body to process.

Crystals & Stones: In today's fast paced world, many of us are deeply lacking the connection with nature. The art of Feng Shui teaches us to live harmoniously with the flow of nature and the Earth's energy. Using the healing power of stones and crystals is a part of that process. Harmonious Living provides a beautiful assortment of stones and salt lamps to assist others in reaching harmony and balance within.

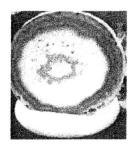

Solar Fire Astrological Reports: These reports can provide insights about your talents, your natural gifts, career choices and the kind of relationships that allow you to give of yourself and to be the most lovable! Location Charts & Astro* Carto* Graphy Charts are also available for those looking for the best place to live.

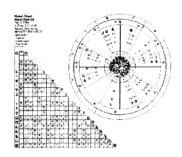

References

References

Art Explosion. Royalty Free Clip Art; (Nova Development Corporation, 2004).

Brown, Simon. *Practical Feng Shui Solutions; (*Caroll & Brown Limited 2000).

DeAmicis, Drs. Ralph & Lahni. *Feng Shui & The Tango; (Core Libre Multi Media Publishing* 2001, 2004).

DeAmicis, Drs. Ralph & Lahni. *Happiness Lessons; (Core Libre Multi Media Publishing* 2004).

Hale, Gill. *The Practical Encyclopedia Of Feng Shui;* (Anness Publishing Limited 1999, 2003).

Jay, Roni. *Feng Shui In Your Garden*; (Godsfield Press Ltd. 2000).

Jones, Katina. *The Everything Feng Shui Book*; (Adams Media Corporation 2002).

Jones, Larissa. *Aromatherapy for Body, Mind, and Spirit*; (Evergreen Aromatherapy 2002).

Nature's Sunshine. *NSP From A to Z;* (Nature's Sunshine 2002).

Schiller, David and Carol. *Aromatherapy for Mind & Body;* (Sterling Publishing Co., Inc.) 1996

Shen, Zaihong. Feng Shui Harmonizing Your Inner & Outer Space; (Dorling Kindersley Publishing 2001).

Skinner, Stephen. K.I.S.S. Guide To Feng Shui; (DK Publishing Inc. 2001).

Stasney, Sharon. *Feng Shui Chic*; (Sterling Publishing Company, Inc. 2000).

Tanzer, Elliot Jay. *Choose The Best House For You*; (Elliot Jay Tanzer 2003).

* 12 parted Euro-bagua concepts and diagram © by Drs. Ralph & Lahni DeAmicis

About The Authors

Mary Jane Kasliner

Shelley Mengo

Mary Jane Kasliner and Shelley Mengo studied the art and science of Western Feng Shui under the tutelage of Drs. Ralph & Lahni DeAmicis. Their studies also include compass school flying star method under the direction of world renowned master, Roger Green. Mary Jane supplements her studies in Feng Shui with a Bachelors Degree in Health Science and an Associate Degree in Applied Sciences while Shelley supports her knowledge with over twenty years in Business Administration.

They practice an integrative form of Feng Shui that includes Classical, Western, Native American Medicine Wheel, Numerology, Astrology, Earth Acupuncture, Dowsing, Space Clearing, Flying Star and Feng Shui Staging and Design. They also introduce the use of crystals and salt products in their work since they are very powerful and essential for our health and well being, not to mention the environment.

They are the co-owners of a Feng Shui consulting firm and Feng Shui school. Their work has been featured in the media worldwide extending their services to individuals, groups and organizations. In addition, Mary Jane and Shelley write articles for Holistic Magazine and teach Feng Shui workshops in local community colleges, community base programs, and small groups.

They are members of the International Feng Shui Guild and continue their Feng Shui education by attending seminars throughout the country. Their work embodies the principles of Feng Shui on a mind, body and spirit level creating abundance and harmony in the lives of those ready to effect positive change.